*Vermont Beautiful*

# Vermont Beautiful

BY
## WALLACE NUTTING
Author of " Furniture of the Pilgrim Century,"
"A Windsor Handbook," etc.

ILLUSTRATED BY THE AUTHOR WITH
THREE HUNDRED AND FOUR PHOTOGRAPHS
COVERING ALL THE COUNTIES IN VERMONT

FRAMINGHAM AND BOSTON
OLD AMERICA COMPANY
PUBLISHERS

THE PLIMPTON PRESS
NORWOOD · MASS · U · S · A

# FOREWORD

THE state of Vermont through its secretary, Mr. Bailey, has issued illustrated pamphlets, from time to time setting forth in excellent fashion the attractions of the state. But it is believed that a fuller treatment, pictorially, with some description of the more beautiful sections will be desired by the present and former residents of Vermont as well as by its casual visitors. With this idea in mind the present book is offered to the public. It is the first of a series projected on the older or more beautiful states, which, if time and mood allow, may follow.

For twenty years and more the author has joyed in Vermont journeyings, and in that period has passed five entire summers within the bounds of the state, besides touring scores of times through its delightful valleys. He would, however, disclaim exhaustive knowledge of any of its features, and if possessing it might withhold it, as information too minute may become uninteresting. He knows there are far more beautiful spots in Vermont than any one person can ever see. Anything that God has made has new facets of light still discoverable by the reverent.

The author foresees disappointment to many persons because certain sections of the state are not more fully shown. It is obvious that one might extend such a work as this to several volumes, but in spite of some regions not being covered, the large number of pictures here included is far in excess of anything hitherto attempted. They are all original, and practically all are now published in book form for the first time. The majority of them have not been seen hitherto in any form, having been made within a year of the date of this publication.

No effort has been made to supply a guide book, but rather the object is to present a book suitable for a gift. The thoroughly good guide of New England, by Sargent, has covered details not treated here.

3

Furthermore, it may be worth while to say that no consideration of any sort except matters of quaintness, beauty, or history has weighed with the author in the selections of pictures or the references in the text. No compensation, direct or indirect, has been received for advertising; all the author has said being just what he himself believes.

In regard to the history of Vermont, it has been so well done that it is unnecessary in a work of this kind to do more than glance at it. All the author pretends to do is to offer as many pictures of Vermont as are possible in this compass, together with such general and incidental observations on roads and natural features as may prove a pleasure or a convenience to a lover of the beautiful.

WALLACE NUTTING

*Framingham*
*Massachusetts*

*To*

## MY WIFE

WHOSE COMPANY ON VERMONT
ROADS AND WHOSE INSPIRATION
AND GOOD TASTE HAVE MADE THIS
AND OTHER WORK OF MINE POSSIBLE

# *Vermont Beautiful*

∴

## I. THE ROADS OF VERMONT

VERMONT is unique in the quality of its roads. More solid sense has been directed to their construction than we have observed elsewhere. It is clearly impossible for a state uniquely rural to construct, or even to plan, a general system of cement roads. The usual thing, however, would have been the building of tarred or composite roads, such as break up quickly and are proving so unsatisfactory in other states. We owe a very high tribute to Mr. Stoddard B. Bates, of Orleans County, for his wisdom in using the materials which he found at hand.

Everywhere in Vermont, except in some parts of the Champlain basin, there is abundant gravel. This Mr. Bates has used. It would be a revelation to some road builders to test these gravel roads, which are not only the best possible at their cost, but strange to say are the fastest roads, excepting only cement. This has been proved by the writer, for he once drove from St. Johnsbury to Newport, Eden, Hyde Park, and thence to St. Johnsbury at a rate of speed exceeding the possibilities elsewhere in New England.

To make these roads so excellent, they must be cunningly compounded of just enough fine matter to permit of packing the gravel firmly. Here and there local attempts at gravel roads have been failures owing to the looseness of the gravel used. This makes a road dangerous to pass over, except very slowly. The beds of the streams which abound through nine

7

parts of the state of Vermont afford admirably screened gravel. There are still some districts in the northwest of the state where the roads consist of pure clay admirable for smoothness when scraped, but when wet or rough after drying capable of testing the character of a saint. All good men are advised to avoid journeys over such roads, because the duffer at golf is a kind, sweet gentleman to a traveller on clay when it has fallen from grace.

In most of our states it is dangerous to leave main roads. In Vermont, however, the roads are so good one may often follow heavy grades over the highest hills, over narrow winding passes, without a jolt or a jar. In fact, a notable feature of Vermont is the generally high character of the minor cross roads and hill roads. It is these that reveal many hidden beauties and characteristic mountain farms, snug, trim, and appealing. There is more human interest in such roads than in the wide trunk lines between great cities. Along them one finds fair homesteads, and good ones, too, at the summits of many of the mountains or lying on the soft slopes at an elevation of two thousand feet and more, for the very crests of the loftier hills are often the finest soil imaginable.

Still following good roads it is possible to penetrate into the very heart of the Green Mountains, which are generally true to their name to their very summits. There is a softness and intimacy about them which is better than grandeur and more comfortable than appalling. They are good to live with, understandable and kindly, rather than mysterious and terrifying. Their glens are ideal homes for common mortals who are not too ambitious, but who love liberty and the sod.

As one goes on through the state a great wealth of beauty is revealed. The main road passing north and south through Vermont on its western side, approaching by way of branches from Williamstown or Troy, proceeds from Bennington through to the Canada line. Its more attractive portions are in the southern half. The eastern trunk line entering from Greenfield and passing out into Sherbrook, in Canada, is more interesting in its northern half. The cross road from Bennington to Brattleboro is very pleasing in apple blossom time. In places it is somewhat narrow. The diagonal road from Bellows Falls to Rutland is beautiful all through the season of travel.

From White River one crosses to Rutland via Woodstock and finds beauty all the way. The passage from Wells River through Montpelier to Burlington is fine. The journey from St. Johnsbury to Burlington also includes much that is good, especially in the eastern section. The most northern cross road from Newport to Swanton is perhaps the poorest road and the least interesting. It suffers the further handicap of requiring calls at custom houses as it touches Canada. It will probably be much better in a few years. The parts of the road in Vermont are much the best.

The series of four roads from the White River–Rutland route running roughly parallel through the mountain valleys northerly to the Montpelier–Waterbury route, are fascinating tours, often neglected, but very important for the lover of nature's quiet moods. Various minor routes will be mentioned in the course of this book, but those already sketched are all necessary to any general review of the beauty spots of the state.

A final rare delight of Vermont travel is the freedom from city sights and noises. One may choose long routes and never encounter any human habitation larger than a rural village.

## II.  THE RIVERS AND BROOKS

THE rivers and minor streams of Vermont are nearly always found by the roadside. They are, therefore, a far more important feature of beauty than the lakes. The unfolding mystery so fascinating in following a stream is one of the chief charms of travel. A lake can often be seen at one point, and is often bordered by a scrub growth. The trees about streams are of a nobler character than are found on lake margins.

It is an odd fact that the use of the word " brook " in America is practically confined to New England. It is a lovable word, full of music and memory. The brooks tell soothing stories, and are better to sit beside than an open fire.

The association of our branch of the human race with brooks is of hoary and unknown antiquity. Before the day of wells our fathers lived by the brookside. There, at five years of age, the boy built his dam with pebbles and sod and set up his water wheel. His sister waded by his side and felt the smooth stones with her toes. The minnows darted between her feet; the great elm overhung, and its water-loving roots formed a seat, when, tired of play, the children sat to view their first feat of engineering. What a brook does not know of botany and geology in its region is not a big chapter. Who has not been lost to the passage of time and the plague of history in following the devious course of the clear flowing water? Here large, there small, now hurrying, now reposing; at one time hidden among affectionate birches, at another time basking in the broad, hot lights of the garish meadow, the brook has more moods and more mystery than a woman.

Brooks in Vermont are as many as there are farms, and every one has a marked character of its own, but never a bad one in the whole list. For pictures, their dimpled elbows and soft reflection call us. They give life and take toll in an agreeable spirit.

More worth-while things can be done with a brook than with anything else. It is easily led; it may be coaxed to expand into pools by the farm-house, or made to drive the old saw mill, or to water the garden. A bridge over a brook is one of the first pieces of architecture, and the prettiest. A man may own much, but unless he owns a brook he is poor.

The Vermont brook is a varying personality, and has its mad as well as its lucid intervals. Indeed, one of the beautiful streams of Vermont is called Mad River. It flows northerly, entering the Winooski in Middlesex.

The Vermont farmer knew how to use the brook in all its moods. In March, when the farm work did not press, he found even a normally small brook swollen to such proportions as to be ample for his sawing and grinding. So he harnessed it for this purpose, and a mill arose to do his

bidding. Vermont must contain thousands of old abandoned mills which give evidence of how a stream was used. They make a characteristic feature of the state, and are one more mark of the independence of the small community in old New England. Instead of drawing logs a long way to a large central mill, the small farmer wrought at home. He cut his own timber, sawed it at his little mill, and built his own barn, which was a big one.

Lanier makes use of the brook as having a purpose, and we are just awakening to the endless uses of water. Vast reservoirs are now established in and about Wilmington whose brooks are pictured on pages 24 and 167. But besides the storage in reservoirs, when water is put to the uses it should be, then Vermont and the states of kindred contour will come into their own. More than the mines of our country the brooks will be the continuous sources of the nation's wealth. Every shower will be a shower of gold. We who live where water is abundant forget that a great part of the human race never have enough water. And water for us, too, will prove the salvation of the East. Nearly all the water power is wasted. The engineers' estimates are all too low. When every hill brook has a series of little dams whose power is fed below to one wire, the hill states will rise in importance and become the centers of empire. The brook, then, may become the most useful, as it is now the most beautiful, feature of our country.

The charming turns and cascades along Mad River appear on pages 64 and 216. The Winooski at Middlesex, pages 80 and 159, has a gorge as appealing in color and outline as others that we journey across continents to behold. Perhaps for charm of stream and mountain it would be hard to surpass the route from Montpelier to Essex, where Camel's Hump, as on page 168, shows itself from many angles. The brooks that feed the Winooski are shown on pages 47, 52 and 83. The Winooski reveals its moods on pages 56, 63, 207, and at the bottom and middle of page 48, and on page 168 at the top.

The White River from its mouth upward exhibits numberless curves of beauty, dreamy reflections, shadowing elms and nestling villages. The Village Spires, page 135, is an instance, other views appearing on pages 36, 39, 40.

The upper Connecticut exhibits better known phases of beauty than the smaller streams. " Fording the Upper Connecticut," page 143, shows picturesque cattle, mottled in color, a double team, with the two-wheeled hayrack capable of dodging about among the stones — the ideal contrivance for rough going. The Connecticut has many fair reaches at Fairlee, Bradford, and the villages farther north. They appear on pages 191, 196, 199, 200, 212, 215. Near Brattleboro, with its bald, black mountains, and at Bellows Falls, recent extensive power developments have changed the aspects of the valleys and added a series of new reflections from the hills. West River pictures are on pages 87 and 112.

The Passumpsic is full of charm. From its mouth to its source there is hardly a reach or a bow that does not challenge our delighted attention. Some of these arresting bits appear on pages 71, 80, 120, 131.

The Lamoille bears in its name a reminder that northern and western Vermont got names, as it is now getting people, from French Canada. A fine reach of the Lamoille, on page 71, shows a spaciousness and dignity worthy of a great river.

Otter Creek, on the west of the mountains, being on a general thoroughfare, is better known to the tourist than other streams of Vermont. In various angles it successively reflects in its course nearly the entire range of the Green Mountains, as on page 23 and the bottom of page 88. But its course is quieter than that of any other Vermont river.

The Battenkill flows into the Hudson, and in its name bears the stamp of old Dutch New York. It is a stream eminent in beautiful stretches, some of the finest of which are pictured on pages 11, 15, and 16.

It must always be the brook, however, to which we return in memory, because it is comprehensible and endearing by its very modesty. Unknown to the wide world, often even unnamed, it is " our brook " to

the lover who dwells on its grassy banks; knows its variable voice, now faint, now swelling to a roar; sees the flash of its diamond and ruby waters playing among the multi-colored stones; spans it or fords it; harnesses it and guides it until it becomes the symbol of his farm and the inspirer of whatever latent poetry lies in him. Such examples are on pages 23, 24, 28, 31 and the top of page 55.

In this connection the farm bridge must be noticed as a feature almost as common as the farm barn. The meadow often lies on the opposite side of the stream from the road where the farmhouse is. Many a farm has a modern bridge of some pretensions, or an old covered structure painted red. In cases where the settler saw his advantage in placing his dwelling beyond his bridge, he secured an approach which for charm may rival the subtly contrived approach of a landscape architect.

Before recent expensive road work was undertaken the Vermonter had often to fight his river or brook. It required no small part of his labor and ingenuity to bridge or curb permanently the fickle waters.

The charm of Vermont touring is much enhanced by the road ramps leading to or from these bridges.

The "old red bridge" has become a proverbial phrase. So far have most of us lived away from it, that the importance of its roof to prevent decay and the quaintness of its outlines, flanked at its ends by fine patriarchal elms, have passed from our memory. We are glad to recall and preserve these features on pages 31, 51, and 64.

Aside from the air, then, the quality of which in Vermont cannot be surpassed, a drop of water from a Vermont brook means more than anything else in the aesthetics of the visitor to the state or the economics of the resident. The latter, tracing the brook to its source, conducts the water to his homestead, where the flowing aqueduct becomes so good and important a part of his homestead that he feels a degree of mild contempt for the farm that lacks it. From springs above his valley he feeds house and barn with a perennial cool stream. In the kitchen is often a great open tank whence the water is dipped up in any quantity. The escape thus enjoyed from the mechanism of windmills or the waste of effort in hand pumping carries into the feeling of the homesteader a sense of reserve power. Like the heart beat in the human body, the spring supplies the life of the farm, and the domestic animals are watered beneath their own roof.

The claim to the crown of beauty has been made for the Queechee River, and certainly it has much to commend it. Gathering head on the divide between Woodstock and Rutland, it follows in its more rapid course a fine mountain road lined with yellow birches whose coppery sheen decorates the narrow margin between river and road. In the quieter meadows of Bridgewater and Woodstock the stream bends its glinting beauty, and at its notable Gulf becomes a somewhat impressive vision, as seen from the railway and the wooded sides of the gorge. Some of these aspects appear on pages 31, 163 and 195.

It is these quieter waters, with their long lights and reposeful aspects, that particularly lay claim to feminine affection. However much the masculine mind may turn toward roaring torrents suggesting strength and the natural conflict, it is mirrors that appeal to the mind of a woman. To such tastes the northwestern portion of the state is most strongly attractive. Here the Missisquoi lingers in its plains almost too leisurely. Otter Creek, closing its course shortly after it leaves Vergennes in the low-lying waters of Champlain, is a mountain mirror through nearly all its extent.

A riverside drive, no less delightful, because surprising in its fair revelations, is that which, beginning out of the state, in North Adams, skirts a branch of the Hoosic River into Stamford. The contour of the fine southern foothills of the Green Mountains in that town is remarkably graceful, and when one sees them, as we did, with fairy-like mists playing about them, they become a revelation of cool purity. Going on to Heartwellville and Readsboro we come on the west branch of the Deerfield River. Some of the slack waters of this branch, more properly confined reserves, nestle like deep-set gems, and attract great ad-

miration. At times, again, the stream breaks for long reaches into white water. Crossing over then to Whitingham, where immense reservoirs are to be created, one goes on to Jacksonville and follows down the North River to Coleraine and Shelburne Falls. There, on the Buckland side, is a prodigious power development. The entire route, though beginning and ending outside our chosen state, reveals its chief beauties within the bounds of Vermont. The journey south from Jacksonville reveals here a deep gorge, with vast boulders fighting the current; there, more open cascades, almost continuous for miles. It is not too much to say that immediately after such a drive one gives way to raptures and can think of little else than the beauty he has seen. This is especially true if the journey is made in a time of high water. The fantastic shapes of the breaking current, the quaint forms of the rocks, the color and extent of the lichen-covered cliffs, the sturdy but graceful overhanging birches and maples, cause one's eyes to wander delightedly from one charm to another, each seeking to excel. The general effect is a richness of appeal that gives the mind a sense of possessing all good things in a moment. To us, this region, not too vast, not over advertised, has attractions exceeding the Mohawk trail. There is not such a crush of vehicles. One feels withdrawn to commune with gentler and nearer beauty, in quiet and sweetness.

The southern portion of Vermont is notable for its many fine rapid streams. The fall is so great, taken in the course of a mile or two, that these streams are a challenge to this generation, for their " white coal " possibilities. The outcome of enterprises resulting in many reservoirs adds very substantially to the number of lakes in the state, as at Rayponda, for instance. Incidently the new water margins running into long valleys and about the buttresses of the hills have appreciably enhanced the beauty of the region, adding charm where in some cases there was only a humdrum denuded landscape. It is the policy of the projectors of these reserve water supplies to conserve and extend the forests above them, so that as years go on the route lately described, and others adjacent, will become increasingly beautiful. It is yet a district of meager population, where wonderful sites for mountain homes are wholly unoccupied. The Stamford scenes are on pages 87 and 100; the river moods of spring and autumn speak to us on page 187, the top of page 188, page 191 at the top, page 192 at the bottom and page 204.

Such routes, over roads not of the first class, yet constructed to provide safety and a degree of comfort, are the salient features that appeal in Vermont. The journey up West River from Brattleboro to Londonderry affords somewhat similar pleasure to the route just described. To find that there are good roads, rich in various beauties, and yet rather free from tourists is a pleasing revelation.

As one journeys on, various things besides curve of brook, sweep of river, and grace of hills greet the eye. Substantial houses, memorials of the solid character of the Scotch settlers who built them, stand in the upper reaches of the route. The colors in the landscape, too, are noticeable. When the season on the lowlands has already taken on a sameness of deep, almost black green, the higher ridges, as at Peru, show through the summer that pleasing gradation of green in their foliage which we notice on lowlands only in earlier leafage.

The apple blossoms on these highlands trail their fragrance into June, being at least three weeks later than in lower New England and a month behind the middle Atlantic states. If one follows the season, as this year we did, one extends to the perfect seven the number of weeks that the incomparable apple blossom may be enjoyed. The little rivers of Vermont are so often confined between shouldering hills that the orchards are huddled close to the water's edge, and their location thus increases the strength of their appeal. Where, as so often happens, the wild apple springs up, selecting a strategically fine setting for itself, the tired mind loses itself in days of admiration and feels the freshness of youth return by mere repetition of invitation to be a child of spring again.

So the rain and its children, the brook and the river, have shaped the face of the state, the direction of its valleys, and its social relations. They

have carved its curves of beauty and built its stores of power. The green hills give out forever their crystal springs; and water, whether in mist or cascade or at rest, is the origin of wealth and charm to the bounteously endowed mother of men, dear old Vermont.

## III. LAKES OF VERMONT

THE LAKE, which is only a burgeoning brook, needs our glances of admiration as we leave the subject of streams.

Fairer than all the daughters of pride among the lakes of Vermont lies Willoughby, the queen of them all. Flanked by twin cleft cliffs rising to mountain dignity, surrounded by birches, "divinely tall and most divinely fair," colored with a richness no gem can rival, Willoughby became known for its drawing power even before the White Mountains. A great many years ago a hotel of pretensions stood near it, and the sophisticated city dweller came to wonder and worship at the pure, mysterious waters of the lake. But the trend of travel shifted, and Willoughby was forgotten or slighted by all except those few who felt more deeply and understandingly her stately beauty. The completion of a good highway past her shores is at length re-awakening us to the attractions of a lake more neglected doubtless than any other scenic spot in New England. If merit alone be considered, Willoughby should be haunted by thousands, where one now gazes on her as she casts aside her morning drapery of haze or clothes herself in the colors of sunset. Charming from every aspect, each season and each day she has something new to show her true admirer. The climb of Mt. Pisgah, not too severe for women who have the strength to vote, is an experience not to be missed. The writer made it some time ago with a gentleman over seventy years of age, who now, after growing younger annually, still lights his days by the memory of that outing. The author felt no such charm in the ascent of Pike's Peak.

Lake Willoughby, pages 84 and 132, and its roads, pages 60, 79, and 296, while bounded by many small cottages, is still unspoiled by the garish features so objectionably present at many resorts. To the quiet and the appreciative this lake offers pleasures secret and serene.

To the north, Memphremagog spreads broadly her fine waters, and reaches well into Canada. From her bluffs, pages 95, 103, and 119, appear broad expanses to be explored from Newport. Doubtless the fisherman and the sailor find all they ask — or should ask — on her broad bosom. The mountains gird her northwestern shores. The shimmering reflections dance noiselessly, and the colored shadows play over mountain and water until the beholder loses his heart to their witchery and elusive evanescence. Fine outlooks are had as one approaches Newport from the north. Excepting Champlain this is the most extensive of Vermont lakes.

Bomoseen has long been popular. We have given glimpses of this lake from the east, pages 91 and 96.

A little way from Brandon, a pleasing village and a desirable headquarters, is Lake Dunmore. Birches, as on pages 96 and 108 surround it and grace the trails that lead to it; while a drive, more or less near its shores, follows its outline. In its name the lake shows the influence of Scotch settlers, who, by using a nomenclature borrowed from their own heather-grown hills, have given to us romantic suggestions of much imaginative appeal. Other pictures of the lake and the fine birch roads that lead to it, are at the bottom of page 40 and on page 296.

The great extent and historic and present day importance of Champlain dominates too much, perhaps, the thought of the tourist. A sail over its waters, or a view from its eastern shore, gives a noble and endless panorama of the Adirondacks, which are really a more important feature of Western Vermont scenery than are her own Green Mountains. The cliffs of Champlain, page 76, are bold; and Rock Creek Park, also on page 76, borders the shore of the lake at Burlington.

It is not feasible to narrate what rambles about the many tiny lakes of

Vermont the author has enjoyed. That about Joe's Pond, near Danville, is only one of many. This little lake, resting for the most part in quiet sylvan hollows, hidden from the world, pure, deep, and alluring, furnishes many delights.

## IV. VILLAGES OF VERMONT

OF all places the village is the one where human nature is best studied and most thoroughly enjoyed. In a Vermont village there is just the right number of people for each to know the other. Here the restraining influence of the morally sane is felt more powerfully than in any other human community. Very shame, arising from living, as on a stage, in the sight of all one's fellows, holds the naturally unlovely mortal to an outward conformity to common sense ideals. The village may have its miser, but he is not wholly abandoned to his idol. A common need, and the knowledge that all his neighbors know he is holding out against offering his help, is the most moving social and moral force to mellow his crusty soul. In the village, virtues and graces shine with quiet splendor. Here the saint, the nurse, unpaid but loved, the good and well-to-do citizen, all live in the presence of their brothers, like Job of old.

In the village there is about the proper intellectual stimulus to be enjoyable and good for the average mind. The common man there feels the simpler humor of life and responds to its gentle stimulus. Neighbor touches up neighbor with sallies of pleasant wit, not too biting, not too brilliant. In fact the village is a world in a nutshell, with its play of passion.

The quiet sensible villager is under no delusions such as the unsophisticated city cartoonist puts upon him. In his sufficient homestead he estimates properly his own abilities and his relation to the broad aspects of life. He knows himself for what he is — no peasant, no groundling, but an independent thinker, who, while he does not hope to set the river afire, still knows how to keep it in bounds, to use it and enjoy it. He is the salt of human society, the natural progressive conservative who holds the world to its steady course and prevents a too dangerous swing of the pendulum.

Not a few villagers have remained villagers because of circumstances. Often, left in charge of home acres or local interests, they have philo-sophically accepted the duties laid upon them, sometimes paying off from the family property the portions of the brothers and sisters and living themselves on the old estates. This task of making a meager inheritance yield dowries and stipends calls for uncommon ability, such as brainy city lawyers often deny to the villager and attempt in vain to copy.

That the villager or the farmer belongs to a mediocre mentality whose dullness may be the proper butt of urban minds, is a great mistake. By the very meagerness of the physical resources at his hand, the villager is called on to execute tasks that might well appall the brilliant and the learned, and prove too much for a man of affairs in world marts. As a tree growing in the open strikes root more broadly and deeply, and sends out stout and decorative branches, while its forest brother has merely a tuft at the top and if exposed falls in the first storm, so the village dweller usually develops more nearly to a rounded man than his city brother, and sees life in larger proportions. As we look at America's vastest metropolis, developed to over-swollen congestion, we are reminded of the extremely narrow provincialism that commonly marks its untravelled residents. Life can be smaller and narrower in a great city than any-where else on earth. Such centers must be fed by the stronger men like those who for generations have streamed forth from Vermont and have become ruling influences in the cities. But the Vermonter who remained at home often chose the better part. Man for man the urban is no match for the rural mind.

Vermont's only city that fairly seems a city is Burlington, with the possible exception of Rutland. And neither of these, happily, has far outgrown the marks and merits of the village. The entire state is a

succession of communities of two to five or six thousand, each possessing most of those features that make life good. They lack, indeed, in their churches, the brilliant eloquence of great preachers, but their pulpits are occupied by men who think and who make their hearers think. The villager may have fewer books to read than his city friends, but he is better read for having less to read. His village library is digested because it is not too various and huge. He knows the great thoughts of the ages, and places himself in harmony with the life around him. He knows better than the labor leader the futility of political nostrums, tried and tried in vain in all their specious aspects since the days of the Greeks. You can fool a great part of the world, but you cannot fool the typical English or Scotch Vermonter by an argument that anything except character in the citizen can raise a strong state.

This quality of political soundness, such as we saw in Senator Edmunds, and later in Judge Ide, is the emphatic mark of the Vermonter. He does not go off half-cocked. Good judgment, shown so clearly in his home affairs, is equally apparent in him when he goes forth on national errands. He does not grow excited. Like Dewey, who calmly ordered his officer to fire when ready, the average Vermonter fires when ready, neither before nor after, and with a cool head and untrembling arm he hits the mark, if anybody can.

The good qualities of canniness without its taint of selfishness, of caution that can be daring when it is ready to strike, are admirable features of Vermonters. A Vermonter in a business of some dimensions had with him younger men who carried out the usual routine but sometimes reached for that which might overset them. I once asked this man, after he had been to his office many years, if he still took an active part in business. "Yes, I go every day," he replied, "and once in a while I say No." The quiet drollery of the wise experienced face was irresistible. The strength of the hills is in the blood of these men. They love things worth loving and hate what is hateful. Getting together numerous things and counting the congeries of pelf is one man's life; gaining poise, and enjoying today in such a manner that tomorrow is more enjoyable, is another and better man's life.

How far the land he lives in makes the Vermonter is not easy to say. We know, however, that the man fits the state and that state and man react effectively and satisfactorily. If the state does not form its men it favors the development of those qualities most admirable and most hopeful in citizens of a state which we pray may last long, the stars of its flag still reproducing the beauty and strength of the stars above us.

The mountains, then, of Vermont are not too high for its citizens to climb, its valleys not too profound for them to develop. Its background is one of strength, quietness, and hope. It has mysteries like every human character that is not shallow. It suggests wealth of resource, and offers a theater for courage and hardy effort — the kind of courage and hardihood that is not afraid to do what it were well to have done.

Hence the Vermont villager is satisfied that his home is good and suited to the enrichment of life, stimulative to those faculties which we like to see saliently in our brothers. In his valley, nestled between the hills, he rationally tries to develop that kind of a community, which, to a wise aeronaut, would appear appropriate, learning to grapple human problems manfully, and to leave a memory that will impress mankind with the worth and dignity of life.

Historians have often elaborated the development of the small Greek city, and have found much to commend in the kind of human stimulus it afforded. We are strongly of opinion that a Vermont village, unwalled, tends to build up a better average individual than did the ancient Greek city. The "village Hampden" may grow here to perfection, but he goes forth to stand for all that the original greater Hampden stood. There is no bucolic narrowness here such as delineated in Gray's *Elegy*. There is plenty of timber for a national structure in the Vermont character. That it is not all applied need not so much fret us. The finest use of character is its very being. If Vermont raises men of good bone and fine lineaments, that is what the state wants and that is

what they came into the world to be. If they are not drafted into the broader concerns of life, it is satisfactory to see they are grand material.

The Vermont village has its particularly loved mountain and stream. The sweep of its hill road is photographed on the villager's mind from the days of barefoot wandering. The whole community physically and humanly blends, fits, and interplays. Of all retreats for the overwrought mind, of all satisfactory settings for human residence, the Vermont village perhaps makes a stronger appeal than communities of any other state. Though the influx of the Canadian is changing the better conditions, there are still many places where the race of the first settlers is predominant, and here in a community delightful from its easily commensurable bounds, one understands and places one's self in a cozy corner of an excellent world.

## V.  FARMS AND FARMERS OF VERMONT

SOME years ago the author travelled two hundred miles through a fine agricultural country without seeing anything sufficiently picturesque to call for a pause. But this cannot be done in Vermont. Here is the state of the ideal farm. A farm which can offer nothing but broad acres, fails in answering the dreams of those millions who have, or intend sometime to have, a place to feed their souls as well as their bodies. Vermont farms are so often nestled in a bowl of the hills, and so commonly have individual features which appeal to the lover of home, that perhaps they excel the farms of all other states. Certainly all regions with a rolling contour, trees, and streams give promise of rural homesteads, each having its charm. But in Vermont there is such a homestead around every corner.

These farms can be named. What city man would not pay almost double for a place well named? The poverty of names is one of the humiliations of average human nature. How many thousand " Lake-

view " or " Maplewood " farms do we pass?   But here in Vermont is
a constant challenge to name a country place by a distinctive appellation.
Here may be " Dell Dale," or " Green Rock," or " Elm Crest Farm."
On the fine slopes why should we not find " Jefferson Downs," " Manchester Lea," " Bradford Mead? "   We pass daily what could be known
as " Moss Cliff," or " Crag Crest," or " Green Dome Farm."   But just
as a countryside allows fair birch monarchs by the roadside, trees for
which the appreciative would pay a king's ransom, to be tagged with
advertising, so it allows its best rural assets to go unnamed.   Sentiment
in farm names goes far to make the farm alluring.   " Happy Valley "
is found, and " Apple Knoll " may be.   " Westover " and " Eastover "
and perhaps the other points of the compass have been well and wisely
used.   " Elmunder " is better than " The Elms."   And even " Elm-
over " might do at a pinch.   It could be varied as " Elmo'er."   Why
not " Broadoak Farm? "   Or " Leeholme," or " holme " as the last
syllable preceded by the name of the owner?

The flowers and the trees found around a country place afford abundant material for a play of fancy in inventing names.   " Aspenmoor,"
" Maple Hollow," and " Laurel Glade " readily suggest themselves.
A name frankly taken from the family that inherits the acres or hopes
to hold them affords at least a distinctive name, as " Gale Hall " or
" Vining House " or " Marshall Place."   The English are past masters
in this matter of names, as perhaps we shall be when we have a background of a thousand years.   But why wait?   If one effort to get a
name were made where now a thousand strains are endured for the sake
of a farm wall, we might have a countryside like a poem.

The persons who named the towns along the Connecticut in Vermont
attained no small degree of pleasing and historic suggestions in Barnet,
Piermont, Fairlee, Bradford, Ely, Thetford, Westminster, while the
Indian names are usually euphonious — though hard to spell.   Why
should we try to spell them?   The Indians did not, but even varied
their pronunciation until a half dozen, originally identical, grew to be
merely similar names.

But the Vermont farm, still to be named, was not forgotten in the layout of the world's surface. Each of a multitude has a full quota of all the features which enrich and vary the farm life. A maple orchard every farm has without doubt. A pasture — often the most fascinating of all landscapes to lead us on — a wood lot, a meadow, an upper field, an apple orchard.

Farm life becomes attractive in proportion to its variety. The Vermont farm calls at every season for attention to some part of its well-drained acres. The winter has its work in the wood, getting out for the next winter its store for heating the farmhouse. Maple and beech and birch, all abundant in Vermont, are all admirable for their intense heating powers. The old maple that for generations has shaded a corner of the pasture and given of its sweetness in sugaring time must be felled at last. Its finer portions, perhaps, go into a new floor or a turned chair, to call to mind its ancient worth. The gnarled portion on the hearth sends out a fitful play of flame from the knotholes. So the tree, first shade, then sweetness, becomes warmth, and throughout its career unites its destiny delightfully with the farmer and his home. It is a life which weaves itself, man and nature, in an intimate, harmonious, and poetic unity. Indignant poets may mourn that the toiler is so little above the sod he turns. There is a far nobler aspect of country life — that which recognizes and joys in the interplay of nature and man — himself the finest product of her fecundity, but nevertheless not improved by forgetting his origin. The man who knows soils and rocks, who understands the procession of the seasons, and fits himself to take his part at the right moment in their bounty; the man who grows familiar with the form and direction of the clouds over his own particular hill, and tests his planting and his harvest time by quiet but unmistakable tokens in nature; the man who adjusts himself and his labors so that heat and cold, wind and calm, freshet and frost, all bring their toll to him, and autumn lays her crown on his labors, is as content as a mortal can be, or perhaps ought to be.

The farm with its good road; its quick little motor car; its wired and wireless touch with all the pulsing world; its self-contained various wealth, has presented, or now presents, to nearly all children of Adam an aspect too winning to be forgotten even if forsaken.

The Vermont farmer, so far as he can plan his efforts to raise, rather than to buy, animal fodder, has in his rich corn and grain fields everything to produce abundance and a competence. Of course numerous farm journals, edited usually from easy chairs overlooking city roofs, are full of certain rules, following which the farmer is to become the plethoric fountain of all our wealth.

But when that glamour is removed, and we come down to the torrid labor of haying, to the grappling with drenched, plowed lands of planting time and the unseasonable conduct of the year, never dependable for a day, we recognize that the farmer requires more faith than any other worker. But what the broad-minded farmer knows is, that in the process of the years, nature is not an impossible ally. If she skimps during one season, so that the blossoms are frosted, she doubles a good gift another year, and the forehanded and careful, taking the elements as they come, win at last. Those who complain of sameness in farm life, plainly know nothing about it.

Neither is the monotony which tends to establish itself in the life of every woman present on the farm more than in the city home, when modern change is taken into account. We wonder whether the great war, which often drove women into the garden, and even the orchard and hay field, was not a blessing in disguise so far as farm life is concerned? Italian women never spend much time indoors, a fact for which their climate is partly accountable. But they have chosen the better part, and hate walls. There are many things the farmer's wife does in the way of indoor decorative work which would better be left undone. The woman in the garden, mixing the flowers with the cabbages, as they do in England, is a happier woman — happier, at least, in the results obtained.

Turning to economic matters, it is only justice to say that pinching

poverty in the country can, as elsewhere, be soul depressing. Where such a condition exists, of course it can only be overcome by the steady lift, backed by moral decency, of all members of the family. But is not city poverty, in one or two rooms, far more bitter and shameful than anything we see in the country? The country poor get for themselves a limited independence, at least, not contingent on the ups and downs of markets. The peas grow as well in a financial panic as in booming times. Who, possessing a cow and a cornfield, needs to know what Wall Street is doing? One lives nearer the truth and the heart of things who lives on the sod. Whatever of misery the French peasant may need to undergo with his old-fashioned methods, is not a criterion for the Vermont farmer with his tractor and his harrow.

The relation of a farm to the study of the beautiful was well known to artists, who, like Constable, have enthralled generations by their depiction of country life. And today a small homestead, with its stone walls, its generous shade, its flanking orchard and protecting hill, its purling brook and upland pasture whence the cattle come lowing home, is the proper picture of the ideally seated human family. Such a picture appeals to the feelings as much as to the aesthetic sense, and when its appeal is thus doubled it is irresistible.

The Vermont farmer joins with the Maine farmer, in New England, in being solely devoted to his trade. The farmers in other New England states play at farming, but it is easy to tell, even from afar, where metropolitan dollars have tried unsuccessfully to give a farm the true aspect it should have. The first effort of an urban purchaser of a farm is devoted to walls. They have more of his investment than the fields behind them. To be sure they are not needed. But the city purchaser has not yet come to see the primary law, that nothing is beautiful if unnecessary. Cattle no longer wander at will, therefore the pasture is the only portion of a farm that requires a fence. Economically speaking, no farm can succeed if it is all fenced. The fence is a greater item of expense than the farm itself. But the old stone walls, so fast being fed to the hopper of the stone crushers, were built for necessity and were the commonest agreeable features of the Vermont farm. Where they still exist a little attention, not too much, gives them a harmonious aspect, melting into the landscape with artistic effect.

Unnecessary, modern stone walls may be displeasing, but the fearfully obnoxious feature of poles to carry all sorts of wires is the biggest practical question of the farm, if its beauty is to be retained. A few more such destructive storms as we have experienced in recent years may cause the companies that erect these monstrosities to see that, in the long run, a shallow pipe may more economically carry their wires than a pole line. The increasing cost of wood, relatively to metal, will help to bring about this improvement. A telegraph pole is a very expensive affair, and is continually, and happily, becoming more expensive. Perhaps wireless methods may solve this highly important problem, but that it must be solved if life is not to be unspeakably ugly, is obvious. The leaning and ruinous silo, too, built by the farmer who fatuously supposes it will stand, will, of course, be supplanted by the masonry silo, such as we see in France, whence it was adopted.

A striking economic feature of Vermont farms is their occasional circular or dodecagonal barns. A barn with a silo for a hub and animals tied in the circle around it appeals to the practical sense of the Vermonter who thus secures the maximum space for the least material. Another economic feature, and a very usual arrangement whereby the hayrack is driven into the barn by a rising bridge, is facilitated by the sloping sites available for barns. Thus the load is quickly dumped off without lifting, and falls, as from an attic, to a ground floor. The pride of the farmer is his barn. His convenient material for barns saves him from the wasteful stack storage. It is thought bad form to have a house that is not greatly exceeded in size by the barn. Such buildings, with a corn house, and perhaps a shop, and on the edge of the wood a sugar house, are an effective combination of practicality and poetry, especially if well set, amply shaded, or ensconced in the blooms of May.

Equipped with such a farm, the Vermont farmer is, however, often farther from market than is compatible with daily journeys hence. But his products are partly intensive. Of the butter, cheese, sugar, and the more concentrated articles, he can easily draw large loads down hill, for there in the valley is the railway always, and the market town generally. The first principle of the good Vermont farmer is that all the heavy articles should be produced at home and never drawn up hill.

## VI. A MORE BEAUTIFUL VERMONT

THE most exquisite birches we ever discovered grew on a slope looking down upon the Connecticut. Among them there were huge and hoary boles. Below them lay the fallen leaders of an earlier day in orderly and picturesque confusion. A long river reach opened between their branches. The soft pasture sod was springy beneath our feet. The grouping of the birches was perfect; the setting was superior in its attraction to any public park; it was worth a day's journey to view it. The dwellers near it had an asset to feed their souls; it was worthy to be cherished as their most important possession. We took dinner at the nearest farmhouse, not forty rods from our discovery, and while there learned that the farmer's wife, who had lived on that farm all her days, which were now few, had never noticed nor felt the beauty of the birch hillside. It was necessary to take her to the spot before she knew what we were talking about. Such a lamentable lack of recognition of local beauty is not uncommon. We once said to a homesteader whose place faced a lofty mountain, " What is the name of this mountain? " " Gosh, I do'n know," he replied. Of course he was not a Vermonter! Much experience has shown that the finest features of a landscape are often lost to those who live near them, to those who should feel their appeal.

In the search for beauty the prime error is in imagining we must go far afield. We are continually being begged to ascend this or that height for the " view," when from the valleys where we are the mountains are more beautiful than anything we could see from their summits. Lofty prospects may serve to vary our experience and divert the mind, but near and exquisite prospects are more numerous and clearer. When we glance at a distant forest we miss the witching contrast of a hemlock twig when the pale green growth tips the dark needles of a previous year. One elm in the dooryard, understood and loved, is far better than thousands miles away. Ever the uncounted assets are the larger part of our inheritance. People in the south of Vermont will sometimes journey all the way north to see Mount Mansfield only to learn, if they are at all discriminating, that they have passed on their way many peaks more attractive.

Little by little the villages of Vermont are coming to know that the best possessions of their state have been overlooked. With this awakening some have leaped into public view and are advertising their particular region as the rival of Switzerland. As if Vermont had one feature to suggest that cold perpendicularity on the other side of the water!

What can be done, however, to make the beauty of Vermont more accessible, and therefore better known? In answer, there are several suggestions .

For a few weeks somebody with an eye for beauty should travel with a woodsman over Vermont roads, and on vantage points open, at the roadsides, between the bushes, little vistas of mountain and stream. There are many sections where one may drive for miles without an opening to permit a vision of the beauty that flows beside his way or rises in appeal above him. The Messrs. Smiley, of Lake Mohonk, have shown us what can be done in revealing attractive views. They have made every turn on their estates a box in nature's wide, pure theatre. Pity that we must go to another state to find a satisfactory example of doing things as they should be done! There is no reason in the world why, in Vermont, the average wood road along a stream should not become entrancing. We speak feelingly on this subject, after having fought our way through

brush for twenty years in order to see what every interest of the residents of the region should have made it easy to see. If ten per cent. of the sums spent for " publicity " in any resort state were expended in revealing the beauties of that state, visitors would flock to it.

Also, there ought to be erected, occasionally, simple signs pointing to peaks or streams and giving their names. We have been amused to see hundreds of elms on Boston Common marked " American Elm." But on the other hand we have been saddened that the dwellers in regions of charming scenery do not care enough for their guests or for themselves to put up a sign post.

Another moral obligation of every state is to prevent the attaching of notices to wayside trees. In practice the advertiser naturally chooses the noblest trees he can find.

A somewhat more extensive but worth while work should be the trimming off of scrub for considerable stretches along the roadside so that the trees left may be allowed to develop gracefully. There is many a farm in Vermont with a border of birches, which, if given a chance, would shortly double the value of the farm. It may bring a blush to our faces to urge for beauty a consideratioin so purely commercial, but if such a motive is effective, the world will be the gainer. We can state with a sad candor that we cannot remember many spots in Vermont where any advantage has been taken by the owner of the natural material in his roadside border. He will, indeed, often care for a row of maples, because he can derive revenue from them; but he has an opportunity for proving that he does not live for sugar alone, by giving his birches and beeches half a chance. It is not desirable to establish park conditions, still less to arrange trees in rows. A hatchet an hour a year, judiciously applied, would double the pleasure of the farmer and his friends in the roadside beauties that could then be trusted to display themselves.

Many of our railways are planting running roses on the steep slopes of their right of way. These need no care when well rooted, and are said to be of the highest economic value in holding banks from wash.

It is, perhaps, hoping too much to think that our roadsides ever will be treated like the railroad banks; but one need travel only a short distance after torrential rains to see that the gullied slopes should have been held by sowing the seeds of various tenacious plants. The charge upon the towns of restoring the numerous washed banks of roads, especially of the new state roads, is immense, and it is nearly all avoidable. We cherish the hope that self interest, if not the love of beauty, may cause the necessary care in protecting highway property.

Perhaps another easily accomplished work has been overlooked. Here and there various old farm buildings have been allowed to fall to ruin. As a menace in case of fire, a temptation to tramps, and an eyesore to the community, the public should, and readily could, compel the destruction of such property. In more thickly settled communities such measures are taken. We have only to extend the custom, and this can be done with little public expense by giving away the ruinous edifices for lumber and fuel.

Most of our states have such areas of congested squalor, that a vast and perhaps intolerable burden would rest upon their communities should they attempt any wholesale millennium measures to bring back to beauty their scarred and outraged landscapes. But in Vermont it is very different. Very little requires to be done. It is the most favorable state in the Union in which to undertake such improvements. The entire state is an admirable experimental field for demonstrating that man and nature may live in harmony with beauty.

This work is a moral obligation. If cleanliness is next to godliness, beauty is a part of godliness. What deed recorded in a registrar's office gives any moral right to disfigure a portion of the fair earth?

As regards the palisades of the Hudson the public conscience was awakened, and measures were taken to prevent their ruin. An extension of public action in like cases of neglect or degradation would make all America beautiful. It was originally made beautiful. Nature continually attempts to cover the wounds we make, as on the battlefields where

lilies grow. With so much incentive as Vermont possesses in her natural advantages, so largely unspoiled as yet, it would be a crime against the best in our natures did we not attempt to preserve and reveal the graces of her hills and streams.

Fifty years ago such suggestions were ridiculed. But the moral sense of obligation to the world we live in, as well as toward its inhabitants, is being quickened. If we can give much joy to generations, by arranging before their eyes panoramas of exquisite contour, we have quick reward for our efforts, and make life richer for thousands.

Nor are such efforts the rich man's fad, or exclusive privileges. It is the cottage home that is susceptible of greatest improvement. It is cottages that we picture and that people love to dwell upon, and in, rather than palaces, which cannot look at home in any landscape. Such a setting as that on page 295 cannot be secured except by keeping to small scales. As the diamond is concentrated glory, so the little cottage is concentrated beauty, when intelligence sets to work to make it so. This thought compels further elucidation in the next chapter.

## VII. VERMONT COTTAGE SITES

THERE is scarcely a farm in Vermont without an excellent, often an ideal, cottage site, but frequently little advantage has been taken of natural surroundings. In the old days, following the peasant habit of Europe, the dwelling was placed just against the highway, where the rooms were soon buried in dust and swarming with flies. The barn, also, was so placed as to shut off all prospect, though in this respect Vermont went far ahead of some parts of France and Germany, where the compost heap is directly before the front door. But thus placing a cottage is all unnecessary. A location on a birch hillside, with the land still rising behind, overlooking a winding road, a valley with its silver stream below and a lovely outline of hills beyond, is as easy to find in Vermont as it is difficult to find in many other states.

A suitable site having been selected, the beautifying of the cottage surroundings should receive attention. Nature has provided groupings of trees by the side of which a little house may be like a nest. We allow the birds to outstrip us in taste. They must wonder at our failure to make use of natural advantages. Not seldom a new house is erected without a tree near it. In towns in other states such a thing may be unavoidable, but never in Vermont. We should say there may be a thousand old sites surrounded by noble trees, in Vermont, where once dwellings stood. Such a setting is often more valuable than the dwelling to be erected. Trees should not be too near the house, however. They seem to know how to arrange themselves, if we do our part and refrain from intruding on their dignity yet approach near enough to feel their friendliness. Shrubs may be used about the cottage, but they are better suited to the city, where the effort is more to hide than to disclose the dwelling, but a background of evergreens increases winter and summer comfort. Of green grass about a Vermont cottage there can be no lack, for here the sward is green more months in the year than elsewhere in America, unless artificially stimulated. The old-fashioned garden, for those who can give it attention, is, like a Thetford garden, page 196, a heart's delight. But nature is so prodigal in Vermont, that such a garden, at the side of a house with a naturally rolling lawn in front, and on the other side sheltered by trees that, like Topsy, " just growed," is almost too much of comfort and joy for one season.

The following are a few rules for simple Vermont dwellings and their location:

1. They should be well removed from the road.
2. They should never be lower, but preferably higher than the road.
3. The site should be capable of natural drainage.
4. Good trees should be near.
5. The approach should be winding. Straight Dutch effects are not favored in a hill country.

6. Porches ought to be small, and never surround two sides of a house.

7. Since a house needs sunlight most of the year it is better, if people desire large verandas, to build them like an open summer house, detached, or touching the dwelling at only one corner.

8. The rooms should be few and large.

9. The roof should have a sharp pitch, not less than forty per cent. Italian roof architecture is out of place in this part of the world and has caused much trouble. The sharper the pitch, up to sixty-seven degrees, the more enduring the roof, the better the chambers, and the more attractive the effect.

10. The ceilings should be low.

11. Fireplaces, at least in two rooms, should be provided, and their construction, like that of the house itself, should be of native materials.

12. Avoid a multiplicity of buildings in the farmstead. The shed should connect with the house, and all the other buildings should be under one roof; even a wire-lined corn room with a ventilated side can be accommodated in the common barn, stable, and tool house. Thus great outlay is saved, and the artistic possibilities are increased. If under modern conditions a garage is required it should be connected with the shed.

13. Modern plumbing is clearly the due of the Vermont housekeeper.

## VIII. THE TREES OF VERMONT

THE favorite companion tree for a Vermont house is the elm. It grows more gracefully in America than in England, and is the typical tree in the well-watered northern part of our country. It carries its roots near the surface, and sometimes in dry weather their outline may be traced by the browning of the grass above them.

Besides the usual forms of the elm, there are the drooping, or weeping elm, which is very rare, and the common feathered elm. The latter carries down almost to the ground small feathery branches, and derives its name from the feathered leg of the dooryard fowl. It is a very graceful variety and most pleasing. In addition, there is the vase elm, which for symmetry leaves little to be desired. Examples appear in this volume.

Curiously, the elm when growing in a forest, as at Danville where there is the only true elm forest we have noticed, is one of the most uncouth trees possible. In such a situation it has one clumsy branch, like a ship's knee, almost at the very top, and the tree stops suddenly without tapering grace. Wonderfully rigid braces can be made, however, from the wood of this great awkward crotch.

But when, as is usual, the elm grows by itself, or at least so that one elm dominates others, the shapes of its top, while many, are always charming, and some of its side branches are most interesting. The elm often indulges itself by sending out one branch with a quick turn near the trunk. This branch is called " the friendly crook " and is really a characteristic feature. One will see it perhaps once in fifty trees, but when seen again it is so like the previous example as to be very remarkable.

The single elm has a most sentimental appeal when it reaches out over a road or cottage as in Bennington, on page 19, or in Danville, page 295. Sometimes one great elm, as on page 32, at Dorset, dominates the region and gives an effect of real magnificence. At its best the elm has a majesty never reached by any other northern tree, and only approached by the oak. In groups, perhaps, the elm gives the most satisfying effect. Standing about a pool, as on the north branch of the Winooski, above Montpelier, on page 36, elms are a continual joy, and in common with other trees, they surpass gardens in the joy they give, because they are beautiful all the year, even in winter. What can be finer than their manner of draping themselves over their beloved brooks, as at the top of page 55, near Tunbridge, and on page 59 in the same region? Some-

times they open like a window, as on the White River, page 39. Near Brandon they line the road, as on pages 43 and 88, and arch the brook, as at Forestvale, page 123. Again, slender and straight, as on the Swift River, pages 136 and 275, with little spread of limb, on page 240, they seem specially designed to wake our sense of beauty. It was not strange that the ancients fell into the worship of trees, because at their best they possess a dignity, power, and protective character, and have a great age, thus enhancing our wonder at their strength and beauty, which are the wedded features of a true divinity.

Under favorable conditions, the elm lives two hundred years, and even fifty more, but that rarely. Five generations is not a very long life for an elm. The tree plants itself for the most part by the fence rows and roadsides where the blowing seeds lodge. There is many a Vermont farm with a half dozen fields whose old and even obliterated fences are still marked out by rows of elms irregularly spaced. There they scatter themselves lavishly over the pastures, and spring up at odd corners of the farm buildings, and get footholds by the brook, until they give a decisive character to the farm, and decorate as no landscape architect could possibly do.

It is a tribute to the farmer's aesthetic sense that he permits the elm to grow, for it has been shown that he loses ten dollars a year for every good sized elm growing by a plowed field under intensive culture. The crop growth near the tree is atrophied. Happily uses are now being found for elm wood, so that when the trees are felled something of this loss in crops may be counteracted. While in the days of " The One Hoss Shay "

> " The hubs were of oak from the settler's elum,
> Alas for their timbers, they couldn't sell 'em,"

in these days machinery has at least this merit, that it can shape the elm for many desirable purposes and consequently has found a use for its wood. We are glad to believe, however, that the preservation of the elm meant a positive sense of joy in its beauty to the Vermont farmer.   Long may its supple branches wave, accentuating the fairest lands on earth!

But the elm is not the tree that has brought Vermont most fame and most riches.   That distinction belongs to the maple.   It is the sugar from her maples, like the turkeys from her fields, that has attracted attention from afar.   We presume that the maples of Maine and Michigan have sap as sweet as those of Vermont, but it has not been utilized to such great extent nor been so widely advertised.

The maple, however, has made an irresistible appeal to the Vermont farmer for several reasons besides its sugar-bearing characteristic.   He loves to surround his buildings and line his roadsides with these trees for their shade and their value for timber or firewood when old age comes. The tree begins its life as a seedling with the life of the farmer's boy and reaches old age with him.

Howells mistakenly assigns the gnarled shape of maples to their successive tappings for sap.   But the maple is usually symmetrical and never seems to be deformed by yielding its sweetness.   It is doubtful, either, if its life is shattered by the process, as the amount of sap taken from the tree is a very small part of that which reaches its branches.   Maples often assume a conical shape, very striking, especially when contrasted with the somewhat irregular growth of the elm and the always irregular shape of the birch.   A maple top may be a true ball.   Its shade is very dense, and its leaves in spring reach amazingly quick maturity.

The rock, or sugar maple, which forms a feature of farm scenery in Vermont, has a near brother in the water, or swamp maple, the coloring of which in spring is fully as gorgeously red as in the autumn.   The lower portions of New England are richer in the water maple and correspondingly poorer in the sugar maple.   Hard and soft are other names applied to these fine trees, the sugar, or rock maples, being hard, and affording an intense heat as fuel.

During a recent autumn we threaded many roads of Vermont, reveling in the glory of color on the hillsides.   And now, since the discovery of

coal tar dyes, we know that all that splendor of color has been "put down," as we say of preserved foods, every autumn since the maple first grew. Nothing really good ever perishes — some theologian said it, and now some scientist endorses him, and all men believe it, if there is good in them.

It is odd how at different seasons the various forms of vegetation have their "innings" in supplying Vermont with beauty. In the spring, when apple trees flourish, they seem to fill the landscape, so that one notices little else. With the ripening of June, the various delicate gradations of deciduous foliage express themselves with an almost equal emphasis, and the apple tree is unnoticed. With autumn the splendor of color, absorbing all the glory of the spectrum, announces its supremacy over the hills; and in winter we are impressed by the vast number and predominant dark density of the evergreens! Alas for the city dweller, a voluntary slave, shut away from the empurpled hills, the white crests, the joyous march of the equinoxes!

For in winter, too, Vermont is beautiful. A man whom we are all glad to count a friend, Mr. Arthur B. Wilder, of Woodstock, with a true artist's soul for color, has for many years specialized in the study of Vermont's winter moods, and preserved them for us on canvas. So well has he learned the secrets of light on snow, that we involuntarily reach out, in summer, to plunge our hands in the breaking edge of his snowbanks.

But anything said about Vermont's trees would be one-sided that did not give a word in praise of the birch. Increasingly, as one journeys north from New York city, he finds the birch becoming larger, more various in variety, and finally the tree of dainty decorative quality, exquisite winter and summer. This tree does not grow in the south, and the first vision of it to a visitor from that region is like the lifting of a curtain on a new world. It would be tedious, as it is unnecessary, for us to call attention to the complex forms and the innumerable beauties of the birch as shown in this book. It is enough to say that the appeal of the birch was the first obvious call to the late-developing sense of beauty in the author.

We may also point out that the yellow birch, as seen so often by the roadside between Woodstock and the crest as one goes to Rutland, is quite distinct from the white birch. The yellow birch has a bark colored like burnished bronze. The tree reaches large dimensions on the mountain slopes, perhaps equalling the maple, and certainly the beech. When huge and tall it wholly loses on its trunk the ordinary birch marks and becomes dark and ridged by roughened breaks. As the mahogany of New England, it does duty for finishing woods and for furniture. We call to mind a certain plutocrat in New York who showed his friends through his mansion with a wave of the hand at the woodwork and the phrase, " Solid mahogany," not knowing that what he showed was birch. Nor was he alone in his delusion. The average layman in woods will not distinguish between the two, especially if the wood is from the great " black " birch just mentioned. This wood is far stronger than mahogany, but lacks the fine, narrow markings in the grain which is characteristic of mahogany. We are bound to say, however, that for large effect, the birch so often seen in modern doors is rich and very handsome. How could wood from a tree so beautiful be anything but beautiful itself!

There is a marked distinction, again, between the canoe, or salmon-colored birch, and the white birch, and another distinction between the latter and the gray birch. By all odds the richest wood is the salmon birch, whose name very accurately describes its color, when the somewhat lighter tissue surface is rubbed off the bark. This tree was found indispensable to our eastern Indians for the making of canoes, though on the north Pacific they burned and hacked out the great cedars into boats that were almost ships, carrying forty passengers each. Perhaps our Indians could have found some substitute for birch bark, but its admirable qualities for their canoes, and its abundance, induced the warrior to seek no further.

We found many years since a birch monarch measuring ten feet six inches around the bole, five feet from the ground, that is, the waist, where the white ladies of the wood, as well as those of the town, are measured. This tree was the parent of those that appear at the bottom

of pages 60 and 164. Such virile and exuberant trees as the monarch are called " seed birches." This one grew on a slope above the road. Some fifty years ago when the road ,was made, in the old fashion, by plowing, seeds from the parent tree lodged in the furrows on each side of the road. Hence these beautiful children of a beautiful parent. We found afterward a birch six inches larger at the measuring point, five feet from the ground, than this " monarch," but this later find perished recently.

The almost purely white birch, especially when growing in clustered form, or on a stream bank, is startling in its beauty. Those who see the birch at its finest development never forget the experience. One notices considerable sections of Vermont ,where the birch never grew, or has been eliminated from the list of trees. There are other districts where literally hundreds of thousands line the hillsides. Seen at a distance the foliage largely hides the beauty of the trunks. This is so remarkable that the novice may pass mountains covered with birch and not be aware of the trees. In early spring, however, they are most striking ,with their countless white boles gleaming in a brilliant afternoon light.

A single birch often gives tone to an entire landscape. There are abundant such instances in this work. One should understand that while the birch is not a tree of long life the northern specimens last as long as maples. The grey clusters so common on poor land in southern New England are frail and more quickly finish their career. In the higher regions birches even in Connecticut grow to dignified proportions.

A traveller is often distressed by the great woodpiles of birch in Vermont. One feels it is a shame that so much beauty should perish. But his view is modified when he learns that a new growth speedily follows the cutting of the old and that these beautiful round sticks, which he sees in piles, are probably the third cutting from the same wood. There is no danger, therefore, that the birch may perish from the Vermont hills. Its growth is too spontaneous and no cold stunts it. In fact it shares with the evergreen the honor of growing farther north than other deciduous trees.   No blight seems to attack it successfully.   The bark has a bitter quality which apparently renders it immune from most pests. Its widespread diffusion, its willingness to grow under hard conditions, its note of brilliance, will doubtless enable it to continue indefinitely the daintiest feature of a Vermont landscape.

The beech is not so widely diffused among us as in England, but its sturdy mottled bole, and the unexpected twists of its limbs, no two alike, make it a favorite with the lover of trees and the seeker for beauty.   Vermont is richer in the beech than any other New England state, with the possible exception of Maine.   A beech tree as a lawn decoration is only seldom seen in Vermont.   But where it is seen its branching is as fascinating as any tree growth can be.   A beech wood in sunshine, when the mottling of the soil by flecks of brightness matches so well the mottling of the tree trunks, is one of the most delightful visions our thought can conceive.   A wood of beech, birch, and maple, each setting off the other, has a varied charm.   The maple leaf, the white birch trunk, and the contour of the beech are the three fine features.

We have mentioned the trees most characteristic of Vermont.   Certain others are discussed in other books of this series.   We have not taken up evergreens because they do not as a rule grow on good land.   While of course there are many evergreens in Vermont, the state is not noted for its soft woods.   The poplar is a cousin, and often near companion of the birch — a poor relation.   The oak is not a marked feature of Vermont landscapes, but where one is found it forms, if near the homestead, an important note, owing to its vast endurance and rugged outline.

## IX.  INTERESTING TOWNS

IF we were asked to select an attractive large town of Vermont, we
should perhaps name St. Johnsbury.  This community, in its edifices,
its institutions, and its inhabitants, approaches in some degree toward an
ideal.  Named by Ethan Allen, developed commercially by the Fairbanks family, a fine type of the Yankee manufacturer of the days before
the Civil War, the village of St. Johnsbury gives just the sort of environment to make it a desirable habitation.  The broad street, where many
dwellings stand back at a dignified distance, is a fine example of comfort
without grandeur.  While Vermont is too young to possess many good
old houses, there is one on this street, the Paddock Mansion, which gives
tone to the entire town.  It is said that one of the original Fairbanks
brothers made its shutters.  On page 72, we show from this house a
charming parlor, and at the bottom of the same page the quaint woodshed
arches and an old " shay " where children play.  Dear old " Uncle Sam "
Young appears on page 116, taking his leave from this house after a call
on Mrs. Taylor, the memory of whose unselfish character is an aroma
sweetening still the traditions of the town.

Besides having a notable mansion, St. Johnsbury is dignified by several
stone churches, and, through the munificence of the Fairbanks family,
by a fine edifice combining library, art gallery, and museum.  The old
academy is another characteristic feature of this village, being, it is said,
the most progressive, most prosperous, best attended, and for college
preparatory work, the most successful institution in the state.  The railroad and its concomitant evils are kept in a valley below the wide street.
Fine elms abound.  The maple sugar and syrup industry is largely cen-
tered here, and also its product in candies.  The scale works stand by
themselves on a lower level from the rest of the town so as not to intrude
on the residences.

St. Johnsbury is a pleasant center for touring, either into the Vermont
hill towns, of which Danbury, lying next, is said to be the most beautiful,

or toward Lake Willoughby, a drive unsurpassed, or to the upper Connecticut and the fringes of the White Mountains.

It is gratifying to find, also, in this town a good and leavening number of those citizens who embody the much maligned, but absolutely necessary, New England ideals: a live conscience, an active inquiring mind, and a vigorous acceptance of the work and problems of life as they find it. Perhaps it would not be too much to say that such a town in its ideals and its practical influences means more to America than many other American towns of ten times the population. Views about St. Johnsbury are shown on pages 235, 236, 268, and at the bottom of pages 55 and 244.

Among the resort villages of Vermont, where the market interest is greater than the manufacturing, we may name Woodstock as a typical community. Besides being well supplied with those village institutions which make life attractive within its confines, it has a beautiful situation. It lies in a little empire of its own, near the mountain summits and on the variously appealing Queechee, pages 132, 163, 195, 240. Here was brought to its fullest development the merino sheep, the breeding of which was so marked an enterprise of the last generation. A fine type of breeder, and a deacon of the Congregational church, told me with a laugh in his blue eye of an occasion where he was offered, and declined, for a merino ram a price running into five figures. "It was a case," said he, "of two fools met."

The merino, of longer pedigree than that of most men, excepting those who buy their lineage from delvers in old archives, was doubtless the breed of sheep kept by Abraham. The beautifully convoluted horns, the strongly humped nose, the luxuriant wool, the involuted folds of skin, like the carved linen fold on old chests, the dignified and conceited air of an old merino, are enough to call forth a smile of pleasure from the dullest pessimist and to satisfy the most discriminating artist. On page 27 we show Woodstock sheep, in whose blood is enough of the merino strain to refine the wool without losing the smoother ordinary contours of English sheep.

South Woodstock is a wee village, more a cross-roads, whose abandoned milldam, with its mirror-like surface broken by the stones, made a delightful center before the pole evil became chronic. It was more than a score of years ago that the scene on page 203 stopped our touring, by carriage, for the summer. And it was in and about Woodstock that we first made studies of birches, elms, and pastoral scenes, the last of which, on page 260, called " Feminine Curiosity," had a considerable vogue in its day. The sprightly, deer-like alertness of Jersey cows was caught just as they stopped to inspect us in their path. The fine shady drives of the upper Queechee, with their coppery birches, as on page 31 at the bottom; the old covered bridges at the top of the same page; the birches on page 28; the farm bridge arches on the right of the same page; and the haying scene at the bottom, are all about Woodstock, as are also the pictures of the doorway and the old stagecoach with its wedding party, on page 35.

In Bennington-on-the-Hill we find the best type, perhaps, of the little quiet village, no longer engaged in the world's strenuous activities, yet having a large share of dwellers who have made their mark and are perhaps now crystallizing their experiences.

Windsor claims attention from its age, which, while not hoary, may seem old by comparison with other Vermont towns. Here is Constitution House, an edifice less important architectually than as the birthplace of an independent American republic. As one goes up the hill in Windsor he sees large square houses and a village reminiscent of the better old villages of the Bay State. Windsor has the advantage of contiguity to the fine reaches, north and south, of the Connecticut, and the colony of artists and authors on its shores. Also, Windsor being large enough for good society and near enough to the fine hill country to the west, is a type somewhat like St. Johnsbury, in the character of the men who molded it and in the region that surrounds it.

Continuing our survey of the towns of Vermont, Brattleboro, as the successor of Fort Dummer, the first military outpost of the English in the state, and as the first town of considerable size in the southeast, claims our interest. It was for four years the residence of Rudyard Kipling, whose wife, Caroline Balestier, was born here. The famous "Jungle Books" were begun in Brattleboro. The back country is charming always, but particularly in apple blossom time. On a hill three miles north of the town Kipling built his bungalow, "Naulahka," named for the book written in collaboration with Wolcott Balestier, his wife's brother.

Brandon, many miles northwest of Brattleboro, lies on a plain. It is a place not too large for every man to know his neighbor, and is one of the most beautiful centers in the state. It is prepared to make a visitor's stay there agreeable, either temporarily or permanently. Its roads following Otter Creek are fine, from the number of fascinating view-points they afford. One can approach from Brandon by short and desirable drives the lake region of Dunmore, with its innumerable birches and its reflected mountains. Two roads from Dunmore to the north are available and worth following, besides the roads to Rutland, Bomoseen, and that directly eastward into the mountains.

Manchester is the center of an increasingly fashionable and wealthy set, who have been attracted by the cool airs which draw through its high valley, and by the real magnificence of its mountains. Equinox, page 20, and Dorset Mountain, a little to the north, page 21, are each so fine that they give one more than his share of beauty. The golf links lie circuited by views of these and other peaks.

The stranger in Manchester is startled by the white marble sidewalks, flanked by deep green. Marble is here the most abundant stone. Dorset Mountain, in fact, is composed of marble. Taken in conjunction with the town of Dorset the region about Manchester provides all sorts of aids and comforts for lovers of natural beauty. Dorset village, page 227, is strategically situated for catching all natural delights, as it lies in fair meadows dominated by rounded mountain crests. The Battenkill, which flows through Dorset, is a stream of alluring curves and cool wooded intervals. The clouds above the Battenkill are often glorious. The picture, page 15, taken at Arlington, a few miles below Manchester, gives

a vague idea of some of their forms. The sheltered portion of the river is shown on page 16.

In the northern part of Vermont we find such towns as St. Albans, Swanton, on the edge of Quebec, and Essex. As one goes east, with Lake Champlain to the west, no story is needed to call attention to beautiful outlooks. Of course if one wishes to harbor in cities, Burlington in the north, and Rutland in the center of the state, are the points for excursions everywhere.

Burlington has been called the wealthiest, the finest, and the fairest city of its size. The cliff drives near the city afford impressive evidence that one need not go to the sea for wild and bold headlands, for Champlain beats vigorously at times against massive crags, as on pages 76 and 255, whose beetling brows of rock advance as if glorying in the eternal conflict.

In the drives through Rock Park, Burlington possesses a truly remarkable asset of rugged ledges and splendid old forest trees. In the gorge of the Winooski, page 207, near Burlington, we have a fine series of parallel rock walls where the water has used its playthings, the small boulders, to grind away the barriers. In fact those who love to see water at work of its own free will, find in several Vermont streams the action going on whereby huge pot holes are still forming, the stones whirling about in the deep kettles of solid rock, until at last one wall approaches and breaks down another and the gorge is cut deeper. The geologist can find matter of delight here in the Winooski and the picture lover is no less taken up with the fantastic outlines, the seamed walls, the dashing waters, and the changeful color.

Other notable places in Vermont are Middlebury and Northfield, types of those American villages which rejoice in making homes for smaller colleges with the superior advantages of intimate relations impossible in universities. Bellows Falls, in the township of Rockingham, surrounded by a country of rolling contours where hill farms are picturesque to a degree, is itself busy with manufacturing interests. In Rockingham

Center we find an historical old place of worship, the " meeting house," two stories high, with many windows each containing forty lights.   West of Bellows Falls is the fair village of Saxtons River with its academy, while to the north lie White River Junction and Hartford, the latter an excellent example of a town of old traditions and well-kept lawns.

It would be superfluous to mention all the little centers of delight in Vermont, and even if this small book were expanded to many volumes one could scarcely stand at all the angles of affection from which the reader has already surmised the author has scanned this state.   But at least two towns, Montpelier and Waterbury, may be coupled to illustrate the attractions of the river banks.

Montpelier impresses one as having an extraordinary number of solid edifices in proportion to its size.   This may arise partly from the wealth that has been gathered here as the home town of insurance companies; partly because it is the capital of the state; partly owing to the character of its settlers.   Montpelier's State House looks out on grounds as good in their way as one could wish.   The Winooski is so beautiful, as soon as its waters are freed from the business district, as to be a type of all that is best in a small river.   It flows as if designed expressly to elicit our admiration (page 168), and as one follows its north branch there are an equal number of graces which call for a long pause at every turn and every crest of the road.   On page 36 is shown a pool with elms.   Page 52 gives us another pool, with forest trees and an overflowing cup; also a glimpse of Barre birches; and a curve of the North Branch of the Winooski.   We show additional scenes near Montpelier on pages 64, 203, 204, 215, 216, 248 and 291.   There is a by-road from Montpelier to Middlesex which is beautiful in summer, but exquisite in autumn.   Some of the views of landscape and river just mentioned are found on that road.

The main road passing through Middlesex to Waterbury abounds in interest.   The river at Middlesex, as shown at the top of page 80, has cut its way deeply through the rocks and forms here a romantic glen with the mountains framed in the center.   It was a rough passage to the

bottom of the glen, but it was no small joy to get a standpoint on one of the jagged rocks in the midst of the boiling torrent and answer the wild challenge of its roar.

One can make Waterbury a headquarters for wanderings all the way from Middlesex to Essex. On pages 223, 251 at the bottom, 47, 48, 56 and 64, are some reminiscences of such journeys. The trip to Stowe on the way to Mt. Mansfield, may also come in appropriately from Waterbury. At Stowe we meet as we enter the town a sign: "Go slow, or settle." The period after "settle" is almost as large as the imprint of a man's fist, and was doubtless intended to suggest one. The laconic Vermonter has furnished the tourist a good laugh here, that is, if the tourist is not in a hurry!

On our first journey to Mt. Mansfield to spend a hot Fourth of July we reached the foot only to find a sign on the mountain road, "Automobiles not admitted." That rule has now been abolished, owing to the improvement of the road.

West of Waterbury are beautiful farms, and such cloud effects above the Winooski that painters as yet have failed to transfer them to canvas. At Bolton there are many points of vantage to detain one, the gorge of the Winooski continuing to that town. A swing south to Huntington from the road shows the little tributary stream cutting its tortuous and picturesque course seaward.

One finds much about Ludlow, in passing over the main range, that is worthy of study. On page 176 is a sketch not far west of Ludlow, and at Chester, a winning village, one gets, as on pages 247 and 275, fine specimens of snug farmhouses. Some are set near Swift River, others by little ponds formed by dams. We are sorry to find the word "pond," which was ever in the mouth of the past generation, giving way to "lake." It came to be thought rather countrified to say "pond." But the word is a good one, and ought to be revived. At the bottom of page 44 one sees what roadside birches can do for a farmstead setting. At Cuttingsville, and near it, are remarkably good apple tree settings, as on page 124.

When an old house, possibly abandoned, as on pages 91 and 128, is properly surrounded by apple and lilac bloom, one wishes nothing but to " move in," whatever the condition of the roof. Looking into a cozy homestead, across the water, on page 92, one sees what natural advantages the dweller there has used. Looking out from a cottage door, in the other picture on that page, what could satisfy us more than the picket fence, the corner of the garden, and the wealth of bloom on the old apple tree? How much better than any city dwelling is such a one as this!

## X. CITY AND COUNTRY

WHEN the wrongs of the world are righted it will come about, largely, by perception of what is truly excellent, on the part of the average man. For instance, the family now living precariously in pinched quarters in a city flat will see and know at their worth the hundred thousand unoccupied sites in Vermont, where one may live in the presence of mountains, with the grace of trees; where air and water are free; where the earth is bountiful to the diligent, and where every family may have individuality.

The old English habit of naming a man from his acres, gave him a distinction. He escaped that sameness which marks so many town dwellers, who so far as any individuality is concerned may as well be designated by numbers, like convicts. Are these city dwellers not convicts? Are they not " cabined, cribbed, confined " ? Twenty-four hours strike by the tyrants of transportation would bring each of these city dwellers to the immediate danger of starvation. Life is most undignified when it possesses no reserves. Like the multitude of Rome who cried for bread and the circus, our metropolitan populations are fast reaching a condition in which the theatre and the bakery will mark the outward limit of their interests.

It requires, measured in dollars, at least a hundred times as much in town as in country, to secure reasonable immunity from those things which press upon our human nature and deprive it of dignity, power, and poise. Cattle cars are not as subversive of decency to their occupants as are the subways and elevated ways of our cities to their human freight. As a broad principle, whenever men swarm so as to need to live and move in strata, one above another, it is time to get out on God's fair earth. The crowded populations of European slums come to America, and as a rule seek out an American slum as like that they have left as possible. They have been caught by the name America, where the name connotes nothing to them but plenty. They do not know that the plenty is in lands and room. A ghetto is always a ghetto, on whatever continent. And it is always a public shame. When by municipal regulation a room must contain only so many inhabitants, the law does not go deep enough. Intelligently and faithfully enforced the law would give these poor people a chance of life, liberty, and the pursuit of happiness in the country. The gregarious instinct, bred by the experience of countless generations dwelling in hovels under castle walls, as closely as possible, must be bred out from men's constitutions before they can really be men.

The fine specimens of manhood in Europe, bred during the Roman day, in Germany and on the Danube, had the love of country life bred in the bone. An urban population can never be physically fine, unless every family has at least a detached homestead, an idealistic condition never attained in towns exceeding the village size.

There is at present a broadly organized effort to give the children of the poor in cities a little breath of country air, annually. Is this a kindness? It is meant to be. But the act is not based on a wise philosophy. It confesses too much and too little. The propaganda to get children into the country for the summer, if it is a logical movement, rests on the fact that the country is better for the children, But if better for two weeks, why not for four? Why not for fourteen? Why not for fifty-two weeks? The children are needed in the country. They are not needed in the town. They can thrive and grow up to good citizenship in the country, a thing almost impossible in town.

What we need is effort on the part of everybody to get where bread and clothing and shelter and a proper education can be commanded by the efforts of every family for itself. A good education is impossible in town. There is never room enough for the pupils and they must learn exclusively out of books, or dummy models of realities.

The trend of sentiment is toward the establishment of more city parks. But always the park is far from where the poor live. It always will be. The buying up every other block in a city and making it public land would be a burden no city could bear. Americans are often afraid of facts. But the fact is that the street is the playground of the vast majority of city children. Modern conditions make a parent who permits a child to play in the street, a constructive murderer. To confine the child to the festeringly crowded dwelling would make the parent still more a murderer, and there you have it. There is only one answer to the problem. That answer is, the country for the entire year. It is those who are selfish, or ignorant, who huddle in crowded tenements. They love the city because they were bred to it. They are unhappy out of a crowd. A person was telling the author of his cousin, who went from the East Side in New York to visit his relatives in the correspondingly congested district in Boston. Asked how the visit was enjoyed my interlocutor replied, " Oh! he didn't like Boston. Too lonesome." This was equivalent to saying that there was only one spot on earth sufficiently crowded to enable him to feel happy and to feel at home, for the district referred to in New York is supposed to be the most crowded of human habitations!

It is the imperative duty of all governments to see that the people have a chance of life. It is puerile to say that the death rate among city children is less than that in the country. No sane person can suppose that the torrid, airless conditions of the brick hives of a city can be as good for children as the country. If the city is so good for them, why plead for a breath of country air, to save their lives? This reasoning runs

in a circle and is based on a narrow generalization. Character, manliness, independence, capacity, a habit of thought, all are encouraged by country life.

Vermont is the nearest rural state to the great cities. It offers something for people of every condition. We remember some years since of a farm of a hundred acres, with comfortable house, good barns and other buildings, a little orchard, a sufficient meadow, pasture, and wood lot, on a good road, only three miles from Woodstock, being offered for five hundred dollars. Conditions have now changed. The value of money has been cut in two, and the value of farms has doubled so that three, perhaps four, times as many dollars might now be required to secure a similar independence. But so far as the capacity of every family in America to secure a dignified independence is concerned, it is being demonstrated every day that the thing is possible, and possible without enduring any conditions to reach the desired estate, which are not far less onerous than are endured every day by the poor in cities.

The funds now expended to take children back to town should be expended in getting their parents settled in the country. No man has a right to live in a city who cannot there secure a fair chance for his children. That is a good American proposition, and tested by it and following on it there would be the greatest exodus in human history.

At present the immigrant, if he intends going onto the land, is often hustled out to the barren side of the prairie states beyond the sufficient rain belt. Dumped on a desert, the immigrant is entirely dependent on the railway to bring him, from long distances, at great prices, timber for a shelter. The consequence is the immigrant digs into the ground and becomes a cave man, living in a sod house, nay, worse than a cave man, for he had solid walls, impregnable against the tempest. The immigrant, who going into the west must be a capitalist, must buy every necessity of human life from a distance. Or if he purchases the fine acres of Iowa or Illinois he will find their price ten times as much as in Vermont. And in the West he will live without that variety which gives life its zest — without hills, without stone for his roads, without the charm and wealth of shade trees or forest.

It has been for long a jest to play upon the hardships of those who live on rocky acres. Men, however, go to Florida and actually blast by dynamite a hole in the stone where they may plant a grapefruit! Is it necessary for any Vermont farmer to blast a hole for an apple tree? Besides, as the finest, and ultimately the only valuable crop is men, Vermont raises more men to the square mile, who count in the energy and the worth of the state, than a whole county in Florida. However well men may start in the tropics or semi-tropics, the second generation is of small account, if they belong to the northern European races.

But is Vermont stony? There are many thousands of acres, in Vermont, without stone enough to build a wall around them. As the hill farms go there is almost always enough land free from stones to make a well balanced farm. The stony part left to pasture and forest is all the better for its stones. An acre of good land, near American villages ruled by American traditions, is worth a township in parts of America better unnamed.

The plain fact is, the finest parts of America for homes, for rearing men have been overlooked in the senseless rush to the West, fostered by paid immigration bureaus. New England, from the farmer's standpoint, or from the outlook of the man who thinks of character and culture, is the least appreciated part of America.

In making the bald statement that a good education can be obtained only in the country, we use the term education in the broadest sense.

The greatest American name of our day, Roosevelt, may be thought to disprove our statement. But the fact that he was born in New York City, when considered in relation to his education, only emphasizes our statement. For the frail child was for long periods taken to the country place on Long Island, and his later years on the plains not only gave him strength, but an insight into practical affairs and a knowledge and love of nature. Thus the greatest figure in recent history was an outdoor man.

If the score of successful city men is tallied, it will appear that great numbers — we believe a good majority — were country bred. Our urban life is either hectic or narrow or debilitating. Only strong men can stand it, and the proportion of those that go under in the nervous strain is large. A constant influx of country life is required. It is common to point to the " unsuccessful " rural citizen. Even from the standpoint of financial success, the country man fails less often than the city man, whose business ventures, as recorded by financial rating, fail nine times out of ten.

New York, or at least the cities, are regarded as the literary centers. But while literary workers sometimes live in towns, we often find they were born in the country. In the eighteenth century there were no cities, in the modern sense. In the nineteenth century, the Cambridge authors, like Lowell and Longfellow, lived on broad, ample grounds, really in the country though in town. Cooper lived in the country. So for the most part did Irving. Bryant's love for the country is well known, and he was not only born in the remote Berkshire hills, but hastened back to them as soon and for as long periods as possible. The great names of Concord also corroborate the truth that country life is loved by literary people.

An education, at least in its primary stages, in the country, gives an understanding of *things*, whereas in the city it gives one mostly a knowledge of books. For many studies, like botany, zoölogy, and geology country life is absolutely required for any proficiency. The overweening conceit of the city man, which appeared up to a recent date in the funny columns and comic illustrations, has changed of late to a better appreciation of the fact that the country man knows how to do more kinds of work than his city brother. A man in town learns to do one thing. The farmer learns to do many. He must be a good merchant, as his success depends entirely upon good buying and selling. Inevitably, if he has any native ability he sharpens his wits by the process of disposing of his produce. The decision as to what he shall plant, what stock he shall keep, and when to dispose of it makes him, at least in these matters, a student of men and things.  It is true he may go to bed early, but he has done hours of work before the city man rises, and has this advantage, that he has seen the world at the most beautiful hours of the day.

Politically he has learned much, also.  The town meeting, concerning which historians have said so much, is the means of developing political aptitude in the farmer, who understands and follows up the phases of government in the little.  It is getting to be known that bad federal government springs out of bad local government.  People who conduct their local politics well, are those most worthy to conduct larger affairs.

But there is a primeval, deep-seated reason for the ownership of land.  It establishes the possessor as the holder from the Almighty of a section of His earth.  The ownership of land has ever been the basis of nobility, as recognized by sovereigns.  It is only of late that the distiller and his ilk have been elevated to the peerage.  Even now in England the acquirement of a landed estate is the first requisite to give dignity to a title.  And when all else has been said, at least everybody depends on the farmer.  He holds the situation in his hands, as appears in Russia, where it is found he will not cultivate land if the produce is to be ravished away.

The reader should not infer, however, that the author imagines no good can come out of the city.  The city is a necessary evil, and the master mind in banking, trade, and government is compelled to work from the city as a center.  But more and more that master mind requires the tonic of country air, and the rugged independence fostered by country life.  The Saviour of mankind loved to pass often through the country and consider the lilies.  He loved the mountains, the waters, and all growing things; he studied the sky and the sea.  Particularly in the last work of his life one notices that he went from Jerusalem every night to the little village of Bethany.  One of the finest poems ever written is Lanier's " Into the woods my Master went."  It is worthy of being engrossed in the large, to hang on the walls of every farmer's home.  It

shows very sympathetically the soothing and tender influences of country quiet.

We would like to leave this aspect of our subject with the reflection that God made the country and enjoys it Himself, and that any proper religion suggests a study of and a joy in what is made beautiful for us. All our thoughts should be shot through with reverence at the view of a sunset. We cannot refrain from narrating a recent experience. Returning one day from town we saw in the west a thousand mottled clouds. They began to extend north and south and to rise toward the zenith. Their color was delicate rather than gaudy. They rose steadily, symmetrically, until they covered a third of the heavens. Simultaneously my companion and I exclaimed: "An Archangel's wings!" It was all so noble to see, so soothing, so inspiring. Certainly life seems finer in the country whether it is so or not. Scarcely has there been a time when it has not appealed to the poets, from that unnamed one who told of man in his first garden, to the latest contributor in the local paper.

The day's work is over. The waving grain grows still. The hills take on a darker purple. The sky grows nearer. The call of the whip-poor-will comes from the woodland to the leeward. A delicate soft air envelops all. An apple, well ripened, falls in the home orchard. The flash of a swallow noiselessly sweeps past in the early gloaming. The world is seeking to forget strife and to listen reverently. "When twilight lets her curtain down and pins it with a star," we see in the country a perfect world.

## XI. THE BEAUTY OF A CORNFIELD

VERMONT has an admirable soil for corn, and no finer feature of its summer landscape could appeal to us than a cornfield, well kept. As soon as its waving blades cover the ground in the latter part of July, the successive beauties of the corn begin to entrance us. The pollen stalk raises its multiple cross and sheds its golden dust; the silken tassel hangs daintily from the ear tip; the luscious green envelope, leaf after leaf, folds in the sweet grains. As the season advances, and we see corn in the shock, with the golden squash or pumpkins between the rows, there is a new appeal, a changed beauty. England without this glory of growing corn, lacks much in inspiration for her poets and painters. We await in America those who no doubt will sing with finer rapture than their predecessors the joy of the cornfield.

No food, in a growing state, could be more fraught with beauty, poetry, and the sense of plenty than the corn. The hearts of the Pilgrim Fathers were lightened when first they heard the rustling corn and sensed their relief from want. From the time when the bobolink, bubbling over with full-throated melody, accompanies the farmer's boy in the planting of the corn, to the gathering in, on the great barn floor, of the mellow harvest, the corn supplies us with a sequence of imaginative suggestions. In every stage and aspect it is a delight. A stroll among its tall rows soothes our nerves better than the poppy, and seeing it in generous autumn we have a striking symbol of natural wealth and of the joyous response of the earth to her children. Its long braids of seed ears, hanging on the gable of the barn, as on page 283, are at once a decoration and a prophecy.

Why have not painters used more often the motive of a cluster of corn ears? In both their ripened and their green state they are beautiful. The occasional glimpse of white kernels, where the green husk has partially uncovered them, is not surpassed by anything in nature.

Students of corn say that it has been brought to its present state from a diminutive nubbin ear. However that may be, we know that it responds when we help it in an effort to reach an ideal perfection. By the selection of the plump grains, and by discarding the undeveloped tip grains, much has been done to improve the fullness and weight of the corn ear. Furthermore, by recent adoption of green corn silage the growing of corn has been much increased. As America's indigenous contribution to the world's food store, corn has a patriotic appeal and should be a state symbol.

## XII. THE MOUNTAIN TRAILS

THERE is an association in Vermont of those who love to thread the mountain trails. When, in this age of improved transportation, we are in danger of forgetting how to walk, the mountain climber has a distinct mission to get us on our own legs again. There is doubtless a seclusion and an uplift in standing amidst the vast boulders of the glen or on the tremendous unbroken ledges of the upper slopes and gazing on the world below. A little of the eagle in us all would do no harm, unless we press the figure too far, for the eagle is not on the height to enjoy the scenery.

A good deal has been done in Vermont to make a tramp feasible to the loftier or more beautiful summits. The enjoyment is no less because of the moderate elevation as contrasted with the higher White Mountains or the fearsome white slopes of the Alps. One may take along a guide, or adventure alone, and by the carrying of a modest-sized pack, make camp when night comes. A camera should as often as possible be a part of the luggage. Clouds are always fine when seen from the mountains, though to be in a cloud is not so comfortable, and in Vermont one does not often get above them.

It is too much to hope from our human nature that the average person will become fond of mountain climbing. That is one of the joys reserved for the discriminating few. But in time we shall doubtless get somewhat away from the notion that scooting along the main road is seeing the country. He who merely passes through takes nothing good away with him. The motorist wants to move on. Nature shows her fairest phases to the lover who is not in a hurry. A gentleman expressed one day to the author his feeling that Vermont must be dull. No, the State is not dull; it is the people who fail to see it correctly. The best aspects of beauty are too good to be observable to many. Crashing brass bands appeal to some; the distant faint harmonies of the organ to others. The world is many sided. He who looks carefully will see and enjoy. It is not necessary to throw a flash light from a war ship into his eyes. Let those go their way to whom the best does not appeal. Some tread on lilies; others worship God in them; some love the roar; others the stillness. We get what we want.

The mountaineer discovers some surprising features in Vermont. At the summit of the Bellows Falls—Rutland road where one crosses the mountain, there is a good farm with its orchard (page 100). There are villages above 2000 feet, and some of them are most beautiful. Killington Peak is more pointed and striking than most Vermont mountains, yet high on its sides the grass fields grow, and higher still the trees persist. Except on the very summits of a few peaks there is no timber line.

The most surprising vision from the uplands is the encroaching tree growth on the hill farms. One ceases to fear the destruction of forests if he studies a mountain region. The forests may be destroyed here and there, but they edge out again and cover the land. Districts where once was a teeming farm population are sometimes found now with inhabited dwellings few and far between; for even in Vermont, though perhaps less there than elsewhere, farms have been abandoned. This natural re-forestation of the land is not altogether a misfortune, as the mountain climber may detect. Timber being so necessary it is well that it asserts its right to grow in these remote regions. In places, as in one mountain town, where there are not enough men to officer a town meeting, it is good economy to let the trees have possession.

## XIII. THE MARBLE HILLS

WE have mentioned the great marble reserves about Manchester. On the other side of the state, at Proctor and elsewhere, the marble mountains more largely yield their store. We shall never forget visiting a quarry, more properly a mine, of pure white marble. Its vast dome was

unsupported except by the marble arch left in quarrying beneath. It is an odd and suggestive turn in human affairs that the finest quarries of Italy are owned by Vermont men, who, because of their holdings at home and abroad, can now give one the best in the world of whatever is wanted in marble. It is, however, a still more marked circumstance that marble is never used in domestic architecture in the state. The early development of America called for wooden houses, as wood was the material waiting for use. And as time went on there grew up a popular prejudice against stone and brick on account of the dampness of dwellings constructed of them. Modern methods, however, have overcome this fault, and we may hope that the next great physical development of America will be toward permanence and taste in the buildings in which men live. The Vermonter is rich in clays, ledge-washed stone, granite, and marble. No part of the world is better supplied with the materials for a beautiful and solid architecture.

## XIV. THE GRANITE MOUNTAINS

AS Vermont is foremost in American states with its marble, so one of its cities, Barre, claims to be the world's most important granite center. There is an eternity about granite which appeals, especially among these hills. Granite bears the shock of all climates and suggests a reposeful strength impossible in any other building material. Here and there in Vermont granite dwellings have been erected from irregularly shaped stones — all the more beautiful because not hewn to formal courses. We have even seen lately some stone silos, indicating that thinking men will at last adapt themselves to their environment.

## XV. FOR GOD AND NATIVE LAND

ON page 12 is the church at Bennington, and beyond it is the monument of great and deserved name. The church has a beautiful
lantern and is one of the oldest in the State. Its interior is also very
good. The edifice, standing as it does so near the monument, suggests
the intimate connection in early days between Church and State. The
white spires of Vermont's villages stand beautifully outlined against
the green hills. These meeting-houses, for that was their name, often
provided for the town meeting and other public gatherings. It meant
that our fathers felt no sense of incongruity in settling their affairs of
state in the same spot where their religion was taught. It was a more
rational idea than that which later crept in, that the house of God is
desecrated by political concerns. Our fathers began to govern after they
had prayed. Their surroundings made their manner dignified. It remained for a more superficial generation to count political things extrane-
ous to religion. Even the Romans wedded their government with their
religion, and in their earlier development there was no distinction between serving the gods and serving the state.

## XVI. THE FUTURE OF THE RURAL EAST

ONE can tell at a glance whether a farm is real, in the sense of
being a self-sustaining enterprise, or whether it is owned by a
summer resident. Increasingly our Eastern farms are going into the
hands of those who play with them rather than live by them. This is
well for the neighboring farmer in that it furnishes him with lucrative
odd jobs, for we admit that the city buyer does not stint funds in the
development of his farming hobby, so that it has been wittily said that
the difference between an agriculturist and a farmer is, that the one

puts his money into the land while the other takes his money out. But in the broadest sense, it is a misfortune for any region when its dominant owners do not live on the sod and by it. A sturdier independence is developed by the farmer who must do things for himself instead of being the hired man of an absentee landlord. Some striking instances of this independence have come under the author's attention. In one case the use of a fine farm was offered free to any one who would pay the taxes. There were no takers. Yet some of those who declined to work free acres were ready to buy them and work them also. An occasional city owner may do no harm. He may stimulate the breeding of fine stock, or in some manner set the pace in a department of farm development. Vermont has, however, always stood for its own home-owned acreage. Mr. Vail, whose action is possibly a precursor of that of others, mostly spent his week-ends in Northern Vermont, and has presented to the State his broad lands as the nucleus of an agricultural school. He did much for Vermont. But the average farmer, whose main interests are in his land, will do more, in the long run, than the amateur farmer. We fear the rural East will gradually be bought up by city wealth. Farm land within a hundred miles of a great city is already marked out to be exploited by city capital. We shall have, within two generations, a great Eastern region, such as the district within thirty miles of Boston now is, either given up to country " estates " or turned to intensive market gardening. All the fine sites will at length be acquired, and the physical development of the East will go apace. But whether the character of the new population will be equal to the better old stock will depend on the general moral trend of the age before us.

The English tendency just now is toward the breaking up of large estates. We may hope the American spirit will move in the same direction. Very large farms are still rare. May they continue rare.

## XVII.  QUAINT AND BEAUTIFUL THINGS IN VERMONT

THERE is an amazingly solid bar-post at the top outside corner of page 132.  It is as if the farmer said to himself, like his Yankee prototype, " It should be so built that it couldn't break down. "  He had no doubt been bothered all his days by decaying or tottering posts.  So he spent a great labor in cutting out the holes in this massive stone.  It will be his monument long after the stone placed over him in the cemetery has fallen.

On the same page, at the bottom inside corner, is a long, sheltered approach to a fine homestead in Shelburne.  It is merely a sod walk, but the effect as one looks deeply in, is good, and the fine evergreens are a sure protection against the winter storms.  On the other side the house looks out on a fine panorama of mountains, Mansfield and Camel's Hump among them.

The birch drive on the same page is the beautiful approach to the Robert Lincoln place in Manchester.  The apple orchard is in Sherburne, the town where the fine acres of the Webb place are situated.

" Village Spires," page 135, is one of the best examples of the Vermont village as seen across the White River in Royalton.  The stream along here teems with beauty.

The " Old Red School House " appears on page 139.  It is on the so-called Sandwich Drive, west of Manchester.

" Paradise Valley " on the same page is a dear little river scene, with the farmhouse opposite, on the Montpelier–Middlesex road.

At the side, down page 140, where two ladies in similar garb greet us, the scene is in Manchester.  Opposite is the " Day in June," the background being the fine old Governor Smith house in Vergennes.  The lady wears one of the wedding gowns of an earlier generation of residents.  The family, whose seat is now St. Albans, still continues a strong social force in the state.

"Wilburton Slopes," a sheep pasture at Manchester, on page 172, represents what is being done in sheep raising by a gentleman who is developing an ideal farm, where there are pictures in every field.

Those who love mountains will be won by "Ascutney Meadows" at the top of page 195. There had been a very heavy rain, which gave us a chance, before the water drained from the meadows, to secure this view of Ascutney, a satisfactory picture of which is difficult to obtain. Situated near Windsor and the Cornish colony, and on the way to Woodstock, Ascutney has many faithful lovers. It is the dominant peak of the region, and well deserves all the affection it has gained.

In "A Fairlee Shore," page 199, we have the water-side birch cluster in perfection. Fairlee and Thetford in their names, their location (heads in the hills and feet laved by the Connecticut), and their people, are among the most delightful country towns in America. Almost too small in population to be called villages, too rich in fair countrysides to allow us to escape their thrall, every memory of them draws us back to their welcoming hills.

On page 200 we look up the fair stretch of the Connecticut at Thetford, and at the bottom of the same page is a delightful road in the same town.

The "Faithful Oxen," on page 208, is the only picture in this book which the author did not make. This genial pair, friends of men, had been so long well-trained companions, that they could be driven without a yoke. The kind gentleman who supplied this picture is lost to the author's ken, and his name is lost, but he must have been a lover of animals and must have enjoyed his work. In "Better than Mowing," page 220, we have a man who, tempted by the leaping trout, has stuck his scythe snath in the soft earth and yielded to the lure of the brook, Dorset being in the background.

## XVIII. VERMONT IN WINTER

WE have never been able to interest the public in winter pictures. This is inexplicable, for there is beauty in the snow, and there has come to be a fad for winter sports. Vermont hotels in some cases cater to the love for sleighing, skiing, snowshoeing, and skating. But it is no proof that one loves the winter because he follows this fad. There is, however, inherent in manly natures, a love of battling the storm, and among such natures we may presume there are an elect few who love winter for its own sake.

The curling snow-fingers that depend from the picket fences, the fantastic shapes assumed by the blankets of snow on roofs, the evergreens in their striking contrast, green against the white, are all objects fit to claim our attention. The shapes of large bodies of snow are also arresting. Waves of snow, from the crests of which the spindrift flies, resemble sea-waves with their flying spray. We see fine sand under the influence of the wind assuming the same ribbed forms and wavy surfaces as the snow fields. In places, also, the snow seems to copy the curdled cloud forms in sky. This various beauty of the snow lies all over the country-side, but in Vermont the hills have trebled its charm.

Leaving the beauty of snow in the large, the snowflakes of which it is composed are worthy of thoughtful study. They have recently been investigated with great care and somewhat surprising results. Some patient and enthusiastic student has photographed, under the microscope, many thousand snowflakes. Among them all he found no two alike, yet found not one without a six-sided symmetrical crystallization. These snowflakes, magnified, may furnish endless beautiful designs for em-broidery, inlay, and various other forms of decoration.

The variety of forms of snowflakes is nothing short of a marvel. It would be perhaps a mad reach of imagination to suggest that there are no snowflakes that duplicate one another in their crystal forms. But if in several thousand there are no duplicates, mathematical law would deduce

that there are at least billions of regular crystal patterns! When we notice the human poverty of mind that builds rows of houses all alike, we are humbled by the infinite capacity for variety inherent in nature.

Among these numberless snowflake forms there is not one that is not beautiful. Nature in this respect never fails. The frost draftsman is always artistic, always fresh, always wonderful. Many of the forms would make exquisite lace patterns, so intricate in detail that one would linger long in admiration.

And if nature has given us so many varied forms grouped about a six-sided, crowded crystal, what can she do if she uses all the possibilities in the mathematical mystery box? In the summer we have seen so much of nature's versatility that we think less of it than we should. But that winter, the time when we have been accustomed to think of the world as asleep, has a greater variety than summer of virile forms to feed the imagination, is a distinct surprise.

## XIX. THE MAPLE ORCHARD

WE have said somewhere in this book that the typical Vermont farm has its maple orchard. And the farmer cannot make too much of this grove of trees. Their broad branches tell the passer-by that his land is good, and when sugaring time comes his income from their sap proves in a financial way the value of the trees to his farm.

The making of maple sugar has come to be a symbol of Vermont life. As the syrup has its peculiar delicious flavor, so the production of it has given flavor to all recollections of the state that produces it. But in reality sugaring occupies a larger place in sentiment than in fact. Nevertheless, the Vermonter naturally cherishes the tendency of the newspapers to illustrate and write of the sugaring season.

There is much that is really picturesque in the work of the sugar orchard. The gathering of the syrup, the watching it boil, the uncertain lights at night, the waiting human figures, all give interest. Sometimes animals, too, play a part. The yokes of beautiful oxen we are showing in the stream, were also used in March to draw the sap to the sugar house to which previously they had drawn the rough wood used for boiling the sap.

But the labor of making sugar is very severe, and continues night and day, so that its poetry and picturesqueness are not felt so much by those who do the work as by those who look on. To the children, however, the farm sugaring time is the delight of the year.

## XX. WAITING FOR THE "AUTO" TO PASS

ON page 236 the farmer, more than eighty years old, has drawn off to one side, waiting for the "auto" to pass. The old and the new generations have clashed very sharply in our age. The patient oxen, long the willing helpers of the farmer, useful all their lives and useful in their deaths, must now stand one side. It is the law of change. The man before us was the husband of the woman hand-carding wool, on page 244. She, too, was spinning at an age above eighty years.

To the casual thought it might be regarded as a pity for these old people to toil. The truth is they were very well-to-do, with large sums of money laid away, and they worked because thus they were happier. It is only the sick or the vacant minded who deem it an advantage to lay down the tasks of life and enter homes for the aged.

Perhaps the "auto" will pass for good. The demand for fuel in all forms is beginning to sharpen until we may all take to the woods and chop our own and let the "auto" go. The sources of coal and oil supply have only to become a little less, and civilization's wheel will take another turn; the rural life will be a necessity, and oxen will come back.

## XXI. SOME COUNTRY BEAUTIES

SOME one has said that the young of every animal is playful and alluring. With reservations this is correct. The lamb when very little is nearly the most awkward shape in nature, but in a few weeks after birth this lamb becomes the darling of the children, the delight of every one, and the despair of artists. As for us, we could never escape the lure in the eyes of calves, when, as on page 243, they have begun " to take notice." Always eager, like children, for a luncheon, their " mealy noses " curled as they follow one, always capering in the joy of young life, they tend to rejuvenate anyone who comes near them. And who ever saw tiny white pigs without thinking of a roll of satin? Chickens are of course the adoration of children. A speckled hen, having stolen her nest, came out strutting one morning, every feather standing out, and leading her brood of twenty-two fluffy babies!

Such memories color child life and redeem it from dullness. How much superior are these pets to the teddy bears of the starved child imagination of cities!

## XXII. FOREST THOUGHTS

ONE might suppose, since so much is said of the delights and the beauty of the forest, that the forest would be chosen as man's abode, at least in some climates. But we believe that the dwelling of the pygmies in the African forests is the solitary instance of human beings choosing to live among trees.

Forests are delightful to visit, but not good to dwell in. Wherever forests stand they invariably mean rainfall; hence dampness. It follows that there are periods of the year when a dwelling in a forest would be very detrimental to health. In the working out of living conditions in the country, the dwelling was at first placed in a small clearing which grew larger every year. The settler was oppressed by trees. He thought of them as something to get rid of, like weeds. He burned them in masses. The thought of shade trees came later. It is only as we of the East find the primeval forest almost annihilated that we come to prize it and love its great boles as they appear in Danville (page 268).

There is a strange influence that comes over the human spirit in the dense forest. It is something different from the influence of the ocean and the mountains. It is different, distinctly, from any other human experience.

Bryant has said much to us of this and analogous subjects. The silences of the forest, unbroken except for the soft sighing of the tree tops, is the effect most marked. One would suppose the silence conducive to profound thought, but most persons in such solitudes are overwhelmed by the dignity and strength of the great trees and naturally find themselves absorbed in individual growths rather than in what a forest may suggest to the philosopher. Trees are so filling to the eye, the nostrils, and so obvious to the touch that the lessons of the forest are lost in the forest itself.

But the shady drives are beautiful and are sought out by all visitors to the country. Such drives are those in Colchester, page 224; about Lake Willoughby, page 231; along the West Branch of the Deerfield, on pages 204, 219, 223; or in Thetford, page 200, and along many other roads here illustrated. In fact, the shady spots are, in a hot day, the ones chiefly remembered. They form the most obvious features of country life to the casual guest. In these shady drives the country may be said to be on parade. The " Golden Forest," page 159; " A Marlboro Wood," page 135; a pass in Wallingford, page 127; a grassy drive among the birches at the Bluffs, near Newport, page 116; the farm road heading page 47, in the region of Tunbridge; and the pass of Granville Notch at the bottom of the same page, are instances in point.

The forest is pleasing not alone from the trees still growing, but also from those that are crumbling back to earth, from which new trees arise.

Of course the geologist explains how the slow process went forward, of little trees getting a foothold, and the passing of ages creating wood mold. We still see the work going on, particularly as where, in the higher regions, so many roots are reaching down between rocks to obtain their scant supply of tree food. We never fail to be astonished when in winter we observe how bare of earth are some mountain sides, that are so completely covered with trees that in summer we see no trace of the rocks beneath the foliage. We are strikingly reminded that the trees really live largely on air.

Trees, of course, are always the principal objects of beauty in the usual landscape. Their infinite variety of leaf and of habit of growth, their terrible fight for existence in the storm — a fight which, when the tree is victorious, only makes it root itself more broadly — these are aspects that cannot but claim our interest.

Living things are supposed to be more lovable than inert matter, but there are those who love trees so well that the fall of a tree is a calamity. I have seen a sensible, but sensitive woman, burst into tears as one of the six-hundred-year-old patriarchs of a Washington forest was felled. A great tree is a landmark for miles around, and in England as well as America, a huge oak got itself into political history. The writer of " Woodman, spare that tree," struck a chord to which most hearts echoed. Indeed, one would feel shame were it not so. How much a certain tree, near a farmhouse, means to a farmer's wife if she still lives on the farm of her childhood! It was her shelter, when first she crawled on the grass, and it will droop its branches over her dust when she is carried from her home on the last journey.

The old elm sometimes supplied a crotch through which the well sweep worked. The tree was the first object distantly seen, as one returned over the hills after an absence from home. Its little unfolding leaf marked the time for corn planting. In the long summer days it supplied the much loved shade, when the housewife in the afternoon could sit at her work beneath it. And when its leaves fell and gathered into hollows, her laughing children waded and rolled in the soft mass. Sometimes the oriole had her hanging nest above, sometimes the squirrels chased one another across the limbs, and always, in every phase through the livelong year, the tree had its message and supplied some gift or grace to the cottage home. There are today leaders of the nation who would prefer an hour under the old tree, to any other experience now possible to them. The author remembers a gentleman, said to be the most successful in business and the noblest in spirit in his home state. He came to our homestead and wandered about till he reached the back porch beside the well and the great elm, and said, " Here is the spot where I want to sit for *two hours!* " We are all, happily, so human, and are all nearer to human fellowship when under a tree than elsewhere!

## XXIII. WILD FLOWERS OF VERMONT

VERMONT is as rich in wild flowers as any other New England state, and contains the varieties commonly found in our northern climates. We write of flowers, not as a botanist, however, but as a mere crude layman, who, seeing flowers in passing, admires them, but has made no scientific study of habitat and forms.

Early in the year the most noticeable flower in Vermont, as elsewhere, is the dandelion. It grows most happily near where the human foot treads. It loves to skirt the roadside to be sure we see it when we go by. For it is not a retiring blossom, but as bold as its namesake. It fills some fields with color to the exclusion of almost everything else. Under a blooming apple bough a carpet of dandelions is a vision worth a far journey. One thinks amazedly of the great fields of cultivated dandelions while untold millions of the wild ones go to waste.

The dandelion has the advantage of most flowers in that when it has gone to seed it has a delicate beauty, exceeding, as some think, its earlier splendor. It is as if it repented of its flamboyance, and in its old age

grew spiritual and ready to fly away. Certainly one who should see only its latest development would never suspect that this feathery, gossamer globe, which vanishes at a puff, had begun its career as the sturdiest and least sensitive blossom imaginable. A touch of dandelion was used in the home-brewed wine of long ago. Its flavor was as delicate to the taste as the spirituelle seeds to the eye.

As one passes along the highway the buttercup is next to the dandelion in color and frequency, perhaps. If weeds are flowers out of place, then there are plenty of such weeds in Vermont. We used to be assured that the buttercup gave the color to the butter, but as a matter of fact the cow avoids buttercups. She is a somewhat dainty feeder. We were also told that if holding a buttercup under the chin produced a yellow reflection it was proof that one liked butter! How old, we wonder, does a child need to be to detect the fallacies presented to his young mind? Anyhow, the child enjoys the fallacy while it lasts.

Growing with the buttercup one notices the daisy, that beautiful pest of the farmer. Some inventive person should find a use for the daisy; for, such is human nature, after a traveler has seen a few millions of them, he seems to lose interest in them. Yet they tell fortunes, as ever, and, as truly as the buttercup, can reveal our taste. The great yellow oxeye forms a fine foil for the white daisy. And as both, growing together, mingle in the grass, they are fair rivals of the poppy fields of California.

Red clover is the sweetest, the most homelike, and the most beautiful and useful of all flowers of the field. The bees revel in it and fertilize it; the cows find it delicious. It is good for the land, good in the barn, and good to the eye. The white clover appears more on neglected land, or on stretches used for grazing. But clover must be coaxed. It cannot hold its own unaided against the buttercup and daisy.

The occasional fields of buckwheat make a pretty showing. Their delicate white blossoms send forth an agreeable odor, and the humming of the bees at work among them gives promise of honey and delectable cakes later on. A field of buckwheat, also, by the close growing and shade of its plants, kills out weeds and gives the farmer a clear ground for his next year's planting.

The pasture flowers are not at all unworthy of our glances. The milk-weed, like the dandelion, not only gives joy to the eye but also to the palate. And the same is true of the wild mustard, which is perfection as "greens." Wild mustard in an oat field, however, is no such joy, as the writer once learned to his cost, when an oat harvest became so choked and dominated by the plant as to be a total loss. Another pasture plant that cannot be passed by is the mullein. It dots the barren fields and grows by the old stone walls as tall and stately as the hollyhock. The "velvet plant" the English call it, and cultivate it among the choice things in their gardens, where growing in the middle of a bed its gives symmetry to its surroundings.

About the pools and along the brooks the iris is usually very abundant. It is allied to the blue flag, though "The Nomad," in his delightful excursions in literature and among flowers, states that the iris and the flag are distinct species. However that may be, this flower, sometimes called "The poor-man's orchid," has a grace and beauty very attractive. The pickerel weed also decorates the wet margins, and the arrow-head lifts its beautiful wax-like white blossom among the wet grasses. Growing with great luxuriance by the water's edge and by damp meadows we find the elderberry bush, most beautiful when its white clusters hang like misty clouds among its green, most beautiful when its clusters of dark, juicy fruit bend earthward. Occasionally the sweet, white water-lily appears on still waters. The yellow cow-lily, despised by mortals but loved by insects, is more abundant. As the season advances the joe-pye weed masses its rich colored blooms by many a stream, while the orange-yellow jewel-weed and the cardinal flower look on.

In August Queen Anne's lace — "lady's lace," in local nomenclature — riots with blue chicory and the many varieties of goldenrod where earlier the wild blackberry made patches of white. Asters of many sizes and colors grow everywhere, as well as beautiful grasses which it would be too

long and intricate a task to mention in detail.  We only say that they are almost as attractive as the trees that grow above them.

Some of the daintiest and most beautiful flowers, however, do not come to quick notice but are often stumbled upon when looking for something else.  One day we paused by a sharp cliff, directly bordering the road. While engaged in making pictures we observed a fluttering of wings. Under a little jutting shelf of rock, about shoulder high, was a swallow's nest attached to the stones, and a few inches away a delicate harebell grew.

We do not doubt there are thousands of beautiful flowers of which we have never dreamed, as well as thousands of beauties of other kinds. Those who seek find.  We sit humbly at the feet of every patient observer and wait for words of truth.  He who reveals a new beauty opens the book of creation a little wider and makes life richer and fuller.

## XXIV.  HOW DAIRYING BEAUTIFIES THE COUNTRYSIDE

IT is a mistake to imagine that an untouched solitude is more pleasing than a region where the hand of man has tried to lead nature.  A path is an additional beauty in a forest glade, and a field of corn on a mountain side gives an added attraction to the view of the mountain.  The interest is enhanced by some hint of humanity.

No country given up to dairying — and Vermont is very largely engaged in this department of farm industry — can be otherwise than beautiful.  For the success of his herd, the dairyman is obliged to do those things on the farm which translate the humdrum features of the landscape into something more interesting.  Farms inevitably grow richer in soil wherever dairying is carried on, and as a consequence there is a blend of the better cultivated fields with the wild aspects of nature.

The corn fields of Vermont are chiefly the result of dairying, and also the pasture lands where the roving foot loves to wander in search of beauty. Cows, being fastidious, leave various growths untouched, so that there are wild gardens scattered over the pastures. Sheep will eat what cows ignore, and a sheep pasture cleaned of shrubs and plants has thus less of interest than one where cattle have fed. In the cow-grazed pastures the soft smoothness of the sod is always delightful. The outcropping ledges form seats, an occasional isolated tree adds to the charm, while the herds of Jerseys or Holsteins moving across the downs give beautiful notes of form and color. Most delightful building sites, ready prepared, can also be found in the pastures.

Thus, to the dairy interest we owe varied beauty. To it we mostly owe the visions of hay cocks; of ribbon roads over the farm; of the slow-moving loads of hay, sweeter than any manufactured perfume; of the little private pastures where the calves are kept by themselves; and of all the concomitant variations of farm labor incident to the keeping and caring for live stock.

## XXV. A TASTE FOR THE BEAUTIFUL

IF the Vermont farmer or tradesman were asked what he thought of beauty, his answer might be more startling than agreeable. Yet when he chooses a wife he does so largely for her " looks." The greatest good we can do for people is to encourage them to look for, to cherish, and to enjoy beauty.

The greatness of human character consists in the number of its adaptations to law; that is, in the degree of its harmony with eternal truth. Now beauty is no small component of truth, and runs through every aspect of nature and human life. The character, therefore, that does not apprehend beauty is a very warped and partially developed character. For beauty refers not merely to external form or color, but to expression, to ideas, to the shapes and harmonies of universal truth. No human life, therefore, can be worth much unless it cherishes beauty.

That which is exquisite in beauty is the highest expression of intelligence and power and affection. The best of its kind that appeals to reason is, of course, always to be desired. Through the pagan ages the most beautiful as the pagans saw it was often worshiped because it expressed to the unenlightened mind, as to our own, the best that mind knew. And the ancients were right in that particular.

Our present aim is to make evident how human life in the average may be, and ought to be, enriched by learning to appreciate beauty at its real worth.

The average man does truly appreciate a fine character. But here moral distinctions often become confused, as in the recent attempts to name the outstanding great names of America. Capacity in one direction is often taken for greatness. And capacity in one little department of life, as that of dancing, or singing, has sometimes induced the casting of votes for persons limited to such narrow capacities. As if such persons should therefore stand among the few great names of American history! Obviously a well-rounded, majestic character is alone worthy to be selected among a score of persons who shall represent greatness. That is, perfect beauty, or nearly perfect, in art, or life, is essential for enrollment in any real Valhalla.

But the average person, if he feels these truths, does not usually express them. How far he feels them we cannot know, but we do know that if in the scheme of education those things that constitute true greatness of character are pointed out continually, the average person will at last look upon greatness as something different from the greatness of a conquering general. In Germany the radically wrong basis of education was in setting before children not only an unbeautiful, but even a repulsive ideal.

There is too little exaltation in education of those characters which are symmetrical as well as strong. And in general, applied to material things, the highest mountain, the biggest of anything in nature, is the most talked about, as if mere mass were merit or could be attractive. Mass, rather than form or merit, catches popular taste. That is to say, the taste for the beautiful requires development along all lines at once. It is said one may enjoy anything without analyzing it. That is a misleading statement, for at least the power of analysis must exist in us if we are truly appreciative. The very power of appreciation of beauty holds in it, latent, perhaps, but not less real, the knowledge of what beauty is. This is only another way of saying that the artist can see more in a sunset than the untrained person. Education in the common schools can point out beauty of form and color, all that is visible in a landscape, but often education merely expresses the demand of a community. That demand is not usually sufficiently concrete. But whoever convinces a neighborhood that its roads and streams are beautiful; whoever shows them an aspect of their landscape, a grouping, a composition of any kind, does them a good, and, we may say, an imperative service.

This sort of cultural work among all the people will not be done soon, or ever fully done. But the American who does not learn, like the Hollander, that there is a nobility of shape and color in his countryside is just so far poorer than the Hollander. For if we study the famous paintings of the ages we find that the scenes they represent are not the most beautiful scenes that could have been selected, but that such scenes as the painter had before him he immortalized. Painters are generally restricted, either financially, or by their prejudices or their kind of talent, to the depiction of certain sorts of things only. Thus probably the Holland painter never thought of leaving Holland to find a better or different landscape than that before him. His intensive patriotism, the wonted scenes of his childhood, and the example of other artists who preceded, all tended to keep him in a groove. He finally came to believe that the subjects, as well as the atmosphere, of Holland were ideal for the painter. In his department of endeavor he wrought wondrously, so that now, in criticism, we do not say, What a wonderful landscape! but, How well this is done!

If, however, the American with his thoroughly varied landscape learns to love each one for its special beauties, and to understand that in some

feature, at least, the view from his own door is superior to any other landscape, he has made progress in the discernment of beauty and his life is fuller.

That beauty in our country is unappreciated is proved by the very meager number of American artists who can find a market for their landscapes. The artist is not being encouraged. Whenever a competent artist does good work in America it is only after long years of patient effort that he is sought out and appreciated. Good American landscapes should hang on the walls of every home, as evidence of our patriotism and love of the beautiful.

We hope to see the day when many fine scenes in Vermont will be placed on canvas by hands that combine love and power. But it is a curious and unreasonable thing that artists group in colonies. It would be as sensible for all fishermen to crowd together and cast their lines in the same pool. Artists ought to be roamers. Artists have proved strangely inept in getting to spots most worth while to paint. If competition and grouping of artists is necessary to artistic work, certainly they should have reached the height of their development.

The itinerant postal card maker pictures the schoolhouse, which has no character, the meeting-house, without character, the business block, wholly characterless. This itinerant has neither time nor taste for seeking those features which, lying near each village, give it distinctiveness, which are different from any other spot on earth. For though the human face sometimes resembles its fellows very closely, as in twins, or in parent and child, there are no two landscapes alike, nor any landscape that is twice alike. The shifting lights and the changing vegetation make as many pictures as there are days in the year. The clouds never precisely repeat themselves. There is individuality in every tree, and some say in every blade of grass. Not to press the point too far, we wish to insist on this at least, that the versatility of nature is so great that she never repeats herself exactly, and every spot on earth has an individuality.

This individuality needs emphasis because the trend of government, the easy form of education, and the power of fashion all tend toward a dull uniformity of men and things. Factory products, made of interchangeable parts, are sought to be paralleled in the scheme of the communist, to whom any distinction is anathema. There is a sufficient sameness inherent in human nature. It is emphasized sufficiently. Lack of culture, lack of thought, of care, tend to sameness, and a base sameness. The high breeding of animals is by selection, and by an extreme care for excellence. Otherwise, if this principle were not followed, not merely in breeding stock, but in developing plants, we should drop back to wild conditions and nomad life.

Great men are inevitably individualists in their development, and communists in providing some great good for society in general. A man like Edison is as far as possible from the average man, but the average man is benefited more by Edison than by a million average men. The artist catches the particular glory of one spot — its contours of beauty, its colors of splendor, its mystery, the particular merit or wonder it has to reveal, its alliance with and reach after connection with the universe, and then on his canvas the scene lives for long to inspire and gladden the dull day, in a distant region, perhaps. Thus its beauty is multiplied for the world, and multitudes joy in what at first thrilled only one observant, sensitive spirit. For whatever we find for ourselves passes along, whether we wish it so or not, to others.

The gist of enjoyment in life arises out of observation. Ask a series of persons what they see in passing through a township. Some will be able to tell it all in three sentences. Others have seen volumes. He who saw most lived most. He who sees only fertile lands and herds does not see enough. He who sees only grace and color does not see enough. He who looks merely as a geologist or a botanist sees too little. To be broad enough to see it all, man must be a god. To be so narrow as to see only commercialism is to be less than man. To glory in the acres because they are beautiful, are rich, are lovable, are hiding wonderful truth, is an endless source of large satisfaction to an active well-grown mind. That is what it is to be a grown-up dweller on God's earth.

It has been said that the Greeks lacked a love of landscape. If that be so, the fact is one more illustration of the partial development of all races. That which remains of Greek art certainly has little in it suggestive of landscape beauty. The love of landscape is much in evidence in the books of our later novelists. It has become a fad to analyze landscapes and to go into details in regard to their appearance under certain weather conditions or when viewed in certain moods by their characters. So far so good. But the fashion of noticing landscapes has not sufficiently established itself among the body of the people.

In America the average citizen tells the traveler of a broad view at the summit of a certain mountain road. He never has the nearer beauties mentioned to him. A view is supposed to be important in proportion to its extent. Intrinsic beauty is entirely forgotten. " You can see the ocean from that hill, in a fair day," we are told. Well, suppose we can. It is far preferable to see it as we stand on its shore.

The framing of pictures by the eye, as one walks or drives, is a most delightful occupation. A great camera company is covering the road with the statement that there is a picture ahead. This statement is a great surprise to the ordinary man. Many a time have we seen handsome motor cars roll along through a charming country with never an eye of their occupants turned right or left. God has made his pearls prominent; it is for us to find them and use them. But there are many travelers (we say it from intimate knowledge) that neither know the points of the compass nor even the states they are in. Mountains, rivers, cottages — everything entrancing — flashes by. Less observing than the animals, less thankful, these passengers go on their way telling what Jane said to Kate and what Kate said to Jane.

Some years since we took a party through the best parts of old New England. Fifty miles we traveled unable to induce the party to notice the beauty of the region, and then, judging it was the works of men our guests desired to see, we invited them into one of the important historical museums of America. One accepted our invitation, the other two remained in the car! The incident was a reminder of a country woman who seldom went away from home, but who, being taken for a drive, would say to any observation, " I have to 'tend to my riding! "

So roads are useless, and the fair expanse of heaven and earth, to those who having eyes see not; who have not learned the primary idea of education, to observe in order to know.

If we proceed to try to point out some of the more beautiful aspects of Vermont, we are aware that we can do so only as laymen in art. We leave to real artists the better professional analysis.

The early morning is the silent time of nature. Then, indeed, mists may be on the hills, but as these mists ascend, and before they have entirely cleared the peaks, the views are more beautiful than when every skyline is clear. That is, any element of mystery in a landscape adds to its charm. This is felt in the curving road or stream. As each disappears around a cliff or clump of trees, it leads us on to learn what is beyond.

The element of naturalness, even when we do not secure it in a picture, is still demanded by the eye. That is, a country where every wall is perfect and every homestead like a lodge in a park, is not a thoroughly interesting country. To be interesting it must have something, at least, left as nature made it. It is this impulse which craves naturalness that has of late induced the leaving of great boulders on lawns and allowing wild flowers to grow by them. We are learning to do less with nature. We can never successfully imitate her. If we make living with her possible by leading winding roads through her domain and perhaps clearing away rubbish which, if left, might require generations to care for, we have often done enough.

But besides containing natural objects a good landscape picture must have certain other characteristics. There must be in it a vista, a certain point which leads the eye towards a central object or a central light. Any object looked at square on may be photographed, but such a view does not give a picture in the artistic sense. We get a picture by looking up or down a valley or stream, rather than across.

The matter of detail is also something to be considered in a picture.

A general view is no picture. Whatever mountains may rise behind, there is no picture unless the foreground has some item of interest. One tree always outweighs a forest, for its beauties are more visible. As children stop, look, and listen when you begin your story, "Once there was a man," so the eye naturally desires the concrete, near thing in every picture before you tell it of sky or mountain. A flock of two thousand sheep, scattered over a wide expanse, as we pictured them in California, is far inferior in interest to a dozen sheep near at hand.

## XXVI. THE LANE

THE lane was rather crooked, because there were ledges to go around and the hill was steep. It took a turn by an ancient chestnut that lifted its big, spiral, quickly tapering trunk in a mass of raspberry bushes on both sides of the post and rail fence by which it grew. Opposite the tree, on the other side of the lane, was a comfortably rambling wall of rounded field stone. The rails on their side of the lane had bleached to the color of the stones, and the pale green lichen covered stone and rail impartially.

At the top of the hill the lane widened into the pasture. Wiggly paths crawled through the grass. Over them an occasional apple tree reached a twisty branch. Its petals fell softly from its blossoms and floated slowly away. It was a sharp spring morning. The boy was barefoot. As he put up the bars after the cows he could not resist stepping into the shallow water of the rill that ran near the barn. A crow alighted on a high limb near by. The boy tried on it a pebble from the brook, but with less success than David, though the crow felt his narrow escape and flew cawing away. The boy wished he were a man.

Twenty years after: The lusty young farmer comes down the lane at milking time, and meets at the bars a ruddy girl, scarce twenty, with his baby reaching and crowing and kicking. The soft lights touch them.

They are like the first family, only more daring, more hopeful, and better armed to meet the world.

Twenty years after: Again the mother of his baby girl meets him at the foot of the lane. Little waves, compounded of trouble, joy, and tenderness, chase across her face. "Hatty writes she is engaged. She says her man is good, and his father is taking him into business."

Twenty years more: Down the lane comes the grizzled farmer, and at the bars stands mother, kind, furrowed, but sturdy. "Supper is ready, John. Hatty's boy is coming tomorrow with his young wife and baby. Our children are all gone away, John, but their children are coming on."

They go in hand in hand to supper. It is a long lane. It goes from the home to the hill.

## XXVII. THE OLD CELLAR HOLE

HE WAS past middle-age, and bore on his face the story of suffering, of achievement. He walked somewhat stiffly up the slope near the roadside, and paused by the old cellar hole. Old lilac bushes stood in an irregular row along one end of the hole, and a pear tree leaned over the other end.

The house had gone a good many years before, probably by fire, though it had left no trace except a few blackened ashes. A couple of stone hitching posts in front showed old rusty rings. This generation needed them not, and they bowed somewhat apologetically for presuming to hold their stand so long. For nothing was hitched nowadays. Three short walls of field stone met in the rear. An old maple, deeply wounded where its largest limb had broken off, stood by a corner of the wall. Not far away the limb itself lay shattered. A forsaken lane marked where the barn had been.

The man pushed about with his feet till he found the smooth gneiss stone at what must have been the back door. He gave a poke with his

cane at one end of the stone. He was trying to find the hole where the toad used to live! That toad had scared him a little, and afterward made him laugh, sixty years before, when as a toddler he had discovered the queer thing. That was the first time his mother had let him climb down alone from the door and go about the yard by himself. No, it couldn't be sixty years! It seemed like last week. There were some rose bushes at the other end of the stone. He plucked a bulbous seed from one of them, looked at it a full minute, then carefully placed it in his pocket.

As he stood there musing the lowering sun, looking through a clump of locusts, made long streams of light about the old cellar hole. There was the flight of stone steps where the potatoes were carried down in the fall by his father's big-jointed hands holding firmly to the ears of the bushel basket. Yes, and there were the relics of the bin, under the brick arch. Over on that side used to stand the apple barrels, when his father sent him down after supper with a candle to bring up a dish of Bellflowers or Baldwins. It was a pretty dark place, and he was only four, but he left the door at the top of the stairs open, just a crack.

The sun sank lower. The man leaned on his cane, more with wistful relaxation than with weakness. As he still looked down he spied one or two blackberry bushes right on the edge of the cellar hole. He remembered when father was off at war, in 1862, that mother and sister and he had plenty of sweet blackberries from those very bushes. There were two berries ripe now. He picked them carefully. He took off his hat and looked about, and up and down in the cellar hole. Then he ate the two blackberries. Had one seen the formal way he did it, one would almost have thought he was partaking of the holy communion. But nobody saw him. It was getting late. The light was a little misty now, or so it seemed to the man. He sighed a few times, then turned toward the road.

As he faced the setting sun a look of solemnity and determination, mingled with the light of a longing hope, came upon his countenance. The old cellar hole was left behind him. Camel's Hump looked smaller than usual; the circle of hills looked nearer; the valleys smaller, but more beautiful. Only the old cellar hole looked big.

## XXVIII. THE COUNTRY SCHOOLHOUSE

THE old schoolhouse stood under a huge, glorious, vase elm at the corner where the roads met. It was a square building, with a hip roof and high windows. We could not see out of them unless we stood. There were solid shutters outside to be closed during vacation.

Within, the walls were sheathed with wide pine boards painted drab, as near dust color as possible. The benches were so made that the back of one formed a desk for another. There were notches and strange marks cut in the seat by the new knife. The teacher would have seen it if tried on the desk. The back seat was a plank against the wall. The oldest girls on the one side and the oldest boys on the other, occupied this back seat, and felt a little larger than they would ever feel in after life. The half-man, half-boy, when he reached the back seat was sometimes saucy to the teacher, and then a rather brisk passage of arms occurred.

A barrel stove stood near the teacher's table. The boys took turns in feeding the long sticks down vertically into the coals. The round lid was often red hot. In summer, when the occasional revivalist preached in the schoolhouse, he would sometimes bring his fist down on the then cold stove lid until it rang again. It was the only irony in the sermon, which was usually hot enough.

The pail of water was brought from a farmhouse by two boys deputed for this delightful duty. At recess there was a scramble to get out into the pasture where the ball game was waged. At noon, on hot summer days, we ran a half-mile to the old swimming hole, undressing on the way. It was not a great task to throw off a jacket, a pair of trousers, and a shirt, for there was neither hat, shoe, nor stocking in the party.

The swimming hole was a small, abandoned mill dam. The brook which fed it came from springs, and the water was always shiveringly cold. Here we splashed and played pranks for a long half-hour, by guess, for a watch there was not in this whole party of imps. With never a towel to rub ourselves down, we jumped into two garments and ran for school with the

third over our shoulders. It was a bad five minutes in store if we slunk in five minutes late, thin, white, and panting. "You have been in swimming — I shall inform your parents," came the voice of the teacher. For it was a well-known, well-broken rule, that no boy should go in swimming at noon. He who did so had to eat his luncheon while on the run, and plunge hot into the cold pool. No wonder parents forbade it, and that teachers did their best to prevent early deaths or a race of dyspeptics!

In winter Uncle had white Fanny harnessed in the sleigh. Mamie was tucked in, and the knowing Fanny trotted away to the schoolhouse door and came home by herself. One day a neighbor who lived between the ends of the route attempted to use the empty conveyance to make a call on Uncle. But no, Fanny veered out and hurried on when she saw the presumed trespasser by the roadside. At night, also, Fanny was sent off in the empty pung to bring her young mistress from school. Though there were three intervening houses and two crossroads, Fanny never failed in her fleet errand, either going or returning.

The best of the teachers of this old country school is still living. Though conversant with the wide world and sharing its abundance, she has preferred to return to her native hills. Patient, wise, steady, faithful, she left an ineffaceable impression that knowledge was worth having and that it adorned and dignified life, and that she could and would impart it, whether we wished to take it or no. Her pleasant, prompt voice, her clear mind, her power to make things go in the school, ungraded though it was, all carried weight with us, and we learned more rapidly than ever before or since. For personality in the teacher is everything.

The arithmethic was Greenleaf's. We went through it, and on our cracked slate successfully solved all the problems in percentage and at last the trick sums: found out how much the blacksmith was paid who asked a cent for the first horseshoe nail driven, and doubled the charge for each successive nail; we successfully got the fox, goose, and peck of corn over the river, each intact. We had the six Hilliard readers from James and the Dog — "James will soon feed his dog" (a huge mastiff) — to Marco

Bozzaris. We bounded the states, and drew maps of them on the black-board. We lined up for the spelling class, and went down on "victuals" and were not comforted until we reached home and the real victuals went down us. We were just ordinary children, but by eleven years we were through the course and closed it by parsing, "The moping owl doth to the moon complain of such as, etc."

It was the best schoolhouse and the best system in the world, so long as the best teacher stood there. She began praying; she ended smiling. May the recollections of her old age still cheer her long evenings. We crown her among "America's Twelve Greatest Women." And the hundreds of American boys can say the same of their teachers, and all will say truth. For a good teacher is the noblest of women, and a bad teacher the most pitiable.

## XXIX. THE FIELD OF POTATOES

WE WERE called on to drop in the furrow as we walked, the two pieces of potato. They must be eighteen inches apart, according to judgment, and a good exercise of that faculty it was. The half-bushel basket which held the potatoes was heavy at first, and one's arm ached, but though we had never heard of Aesop and his fable of the bread, it was cheering to find the basket lightening at every step.

When harvest time came, one farmer's boy of six was offered a sheep if he would pick up all the potatoes dug from the field. Six acres of potatoes! When two men dug it was a back and leg ache for the boy, but when one man dug even a small boy had not enough to do. There was time to pause and philosophize beside the basket. The tales of the digger, also, were worth hearing. Especially that cheering one of a man who died from eating too many apples! Not a ray of hope came to the boy in regard to his own fate, for he had eaten all the apples he could find, and never ceased eating except when too far from the tree or the barrel! The autumn

days were full of dreams. Anything was possible on those mellow hill-sides. From them went out the greatest of merchants, the greatest of industrial leaders, and almost the greatest of statesmen. But the highest ambition of the boy of six years, was a jigsaw or a " boughten " sled with good red paint.

Forty bushels was the day's stint of potatoes in the time between chores and chores. The red oxen, Star and Swan, were brought out to the field to draw the harvest home. At the house the little and big potatotes, already separated in the field, went to their allotted places; and at meal time came the compensation for much drudgery when the potatoes were eaten, popping from the oven, with new milk and salt.

But the poetry departed from the potato field with the coming of the all-consuming beetle. As we saw the green plants spreading their leaves over the brown earth, visions of disagreeable work ahead clouded all other pictures. For at first, before the days of spraying, we had to knock the intruding bugs deftly from the plant to a pan and then apply kerosene.

But to return to those oxen. At an age, even tenderer than six, one boy was deputed to walk beside the great, slow, kind beasts and carry the goad stick as the potato field was plowed. At the turning of the row, the boy's heel tripped on the high furrow; he fell backward, and Star lifted his great foot, and even touched the boy's chest with his hoof, but sensing something wrong held his incomplete step until the frightened plowman snatched the child away.

Many a narrow escape occurs on the farm. The classic instance is that of a tomboy of about ten, in the days of the hoop-skirt. She leaped from a high to a low mow of hay, caught her crinoline on a half hidden wooden fork, and hung like a scarecrow for a moment till she came loose, *minus* the hoops. Before she could recover herself and her property, guests of her father, it being town-meeting day, entered the barn. The child hid while the astonished father looked at his little daughter's fashionable habiliments hanging high on the fork. For years after, any unruliness in public on the part of that girl, was quickly squelched if the father started to mention " an accident that happened some years since to my daughter! "

## XXX. THE HAY FIELD

IT WAS a great event for the boy of eleven when he was offered a dollar a day for his services in haying. Ivy poisoned him, blistering feet and arms. The fierce sun of a New England summer beat on him. He must turn the drying grass, rake, and make the load; and, toughest task of all, take the hay on the high mow from the pitcher and stow the heavy forkfuls under the hot eaves. It was a stiff grind while it lasted, and it lasted a month, sometimes six weeks, as one was often " let out," or " changed work."

Once the horses started unbidden as the loader was on the rear of the load, and off he went, striking head-first, just avoiding a boulder. But the big wild strawberries found in the grass, the occasional respite when sent to bring ginger tea to the men, and the big dollar when the day was done, were all balancing joys.

The haying season was the great rush time of the year. Everybody and everything bent to it. And when the thunder heads loomed in the west over a fine field of well-made hay, how the springless hay racks rattled as they were galloped afield! How the men leaped to it, hurling on huge forkfuls! How they tumbled it into the mows and rushed forth again, a race against nature! As the terrible blackness increased in the sky, the set teeth, reeking faces, and tensed muscles of the men responded. The nervous horses caught the fear of impending calamity; and when the last load was hustled in, as the first heavy drops fell, there was ended the most spirited, splendid spurt that was seen on the farm in a year's end.

## XXXI.  VERMONT DAMSELS AND DAMES

WHEN we are telling of the beauties of Vermont it goes without saying that her damsels and matrons are included among the chief objects of interest.  Still, we like to say it.

In school days, when the girl with a long braid of yellow hair came down the road, looking straight ahead, we " passed by on the other side," but not for the same reason that moved the Pharisee.  It was because we " dassen't " cross over.  We could not have spoken if we had tried.  And did we ever pull that braid?  We did not.  As soon seize the hanging end of a live wire!  And then the intense scorn that would have flashed like blue lightnings from those eyes!  The other girl, a good deal older, who freely reached her hand in the games we played — somehow it was no matter whether we took it or not!  Then there was a slim, prim, little Winnie, who would say, " Hello! " in a small voice.  A kindly little girl, nothing snobbish about Winnie; she seemed like one of our own folks.  Then there was that girl who talked through her nose and had a rough skin, who once threw a note saying, " I love you."  She must have been ten.  We boys were nine.  And at once she became the last girl in the school that any boy would care to talk with.  Then there was the girl who lived in the big house on the hill, whose people had a college president as a relative.  She was a thing apart.  She inclined to be sarcastic and no boy could bear that.  So important was she that we never thought of her as any one to speak with.  Once we all stole up and hung a crimped tissue paper May-basket on her front door, and ran a mile like Jehu's horses lest we get caught — a deep disgrace.  They were all lovely girls to look at, and good at heart, though we did not imagine a girl could be kind, who jeered at the boys.  We did not know it was part of the girl's natural armory.

So the years went on.  In boyhood we spoke little to the girls for fear they would not answer us; and afterward we spoke little for fear they *would* answer.  There was an odd repulsion, pride, bashfulness or what not that kept the boys by themselves.  Then there were the young mothers!

How wonderful they were, and how strange that they seemed to love those ugly babies! The older matrons were always so good to the neighbors' boys. It was in meeting these mothers that the boys got their first hint of good and kindly manners. When sent on errands to the neighbors, how we longed to accept an invitation to supper! But of course it would not do, because when we reached home we would be asked, " Well, did you tell all you knew? "

The older matrons were wonderful to the boys in the seeming complete-ness of their motherly nature. The boy naturally feels that a woman, with her kind ways, her large affection, capable of taking in the neighbors' boys with her own, and her thorough understanding of the boy nature, is a fountain of power, wisdom and mystery. She embodies the human race in the rotundity of her attributes. And the country woman, especially, accustomed to do everything for her family, has a reposeful strength very impressive to the small boy. If it is a doughnut or a piece of pie that he wants; if it is a loose button or a ripped straw-hat band to be attended to; if it is a sliver to be extracted; or a lesson in morals to be inculcated — the wants, the joys, and the woes of life are taken to the womanly source of comfort and help. To the boy she is a present visible Providence; all of God that he knows comes from her. This is no less true in the hours of punishment, when the boy is sent out to cut the stick to be used on his own person. For the feminine soul understands psychology sufficiently to know that the chief punishment is the dread that accompanies the long task of procuring the stick!

A country woman, especially in the time when wasp waists were in style, and when frailness of body was fashionable for women, was by her duties and sympathies removed from the thrall of vogue so far, at least, that she was a sturdy woman in body and mind. To her the sculptor must have gone in those days for his Juno or even for his Hebe. Now when it is allowed to all women to be beautiful, it seems odd to remember that the only normal woman in those days was one who worked.

The helpless resignation of the good man to his wife is more obvious

in the country, it seems to us, than in the city. The country woman's complete charge of the commissary renders her more looked to than is the case where the city man brings home the daily driblets from market to make the family meal, and goes to the tailor every time he wants a button sewed on.

The outdoor work, in the last generation in New England, was not shared at all by the women, except as a matter of grace in haying time occasionally. The writer saw many country homes in his childhood, yet never knew of a milkmaid. But sometimes the father would diplomatically approach a grown daughter to induce her to drive the horse-rake for an hour or so, or even assist in making the load of hay. Certain coveted ribbons, or a day or two on a visit to a relative, after haying, were understood to be by way of honorarium for his daughter's complaisance.

## XXXII. COUNTRY COURTESY

EVERY human society worth maintaining has its decent restrictions, its interplay of give and take. In these restrictions, and in certain social aspects, the farmer is much of a gentleman. He may, indeed, be bothered by the sequence of a long array of forks at a banquet, but he has the heart of kindness, which is the source and guide underlying good manners. City folks are surprised to find themselves bowed to on country roads. It is the innate recognition of brotherhood felt by all who face the world's work. The farmer may lack the nice little touches of urban custom, but on his own domain no man is more respectful, for he respects himself first. And he is a good Samaritan, or was until the itinerant beggar made game of him. No hand is more gentle in nursing the sick. Well we remember the tenderness with which a farmer, who came to town twice a week, would lift his invalid niece. She drew strength from his mighty arm, and looked forward with gladness to the hour of his coming.

In the old days discourtesy to women was an unheard-of thing in the better parts of the New England farming districts, and we hope these conditions still prevail. Sex delicacy, so lacking now in our towns, was a supreme, unbroken, and unmentioned law. That element in the male population that might otherwise have transgressed, was held in stern check by the decent citizen, and fear of social scorn was the most powerful deterrent of evil.

## XXXIII. SUNDAY IN THE COUNTRY

THE meeting-house lot was cut out of the big pasture on the hill. Near the center stood the church with the graveyard on one side surrounded by a stone wall. The big corner stone nearest the church had a depression which was understood to be the devil's foot-print. Where he stepped next, deponent saith not. We fear it was in the church itself, because in time it appeared some malign influence got into the old meeting-house. Of course this visible evidence on the stone, that the Evil One was snooping about for his prey, exalted the graveyard into a fearsome place at night. Though why devil's work was ever supposed to be confined to the night, has not been explained.

The minister was a benign, charming man. He was correct of speech, sweet of spirit, and while not brilliant, shone with a mild and steady light never subject to eclipse. His congregation listened to him with reverence as they sat in the white painted pews with buttoned doors. In the gallery facing the minister sat the choir, consisting of volunteers. Though we wished that some had not volunteered, still the effect of many of the old fugues was emphatic and unique.

After the morning worship, an old farmer had a class of " us boys " in the corner by the side of the pulpit. We can remember, now, the lesson which lay " in the days of Herod the king." It was before the time of " lesson helps." The wrinkled, heavy brown hand of the farmer held the open Bible, but the man himself was our Bible. As he walked, thankful

and diligent in the midst of God's works, he was always a powerful sermon.

After the lesson everybody sang that tender song, which ran, as I remember,

> " *I think when I read that sweet story of old,*
> *How Jesus was here among men,*
> *How he called little children like lambs from the fold —*
> *I should like to have been with Him then.*"

It was all, to us, a child, very effective — the influence of really good people, without a particle of cant or formalism. There was calmness; the silence was broken only by the thin note of the locust. Outside there was the wonderful summer prophecy of good, — in the soft grass about the steps, the listening foliage and the intermission of all activity that we might think of our connection with the unseen world. As we trudged homeward, our copper-toed leg-boots in the white dust, we were conscious that the day had much of good and charm.

In the afternoon we used to climb high in a greening apple tree, with a book of stories of old heroes and worthies. Probably the main impression of Sunday aside from that memorable " going to meeting," was the sense of release from week-day tasks. During the week we had no leisure to listen to the outside world. The marvel of this world, when the book we were reading dropped, or when we went to or returned from the meeting-house, never ceased. Every grass blade was a miracle, every bumble bee a challenge to make a philosopher. The clouds strolled at a Sabbath day gait across the hilltops. Beauty reigned, supreme, mysterious, worshipful. A country that God made, and men loved, a country that calls back her children from afar! She has placed her seal on their infancy, and tied their affections with cords like steel. We can never forget her, or her glory and silent eloquence, especially as we saw her on the summer Sundays of our boyhood.

## XXXIV.  THE PICTURES IN DETAIL

IN the course of this book various pictures shown in it have been mentioned.  Here we refer to others in which the reader may have interest or about which further information may be desired.

On the center of page 19 is the view across the valley of the Battenkill at Bennington.  A situation overlooking a fertile valley is perhaps the most satisfactory country site.  There from one's window may be seen the source of much natural wealth.  Mills and city streets, however imposing, never convey the sense of plenty as does a cultivated valley.  Probably the influence of heredity is responsible for the attraction that growing crops exert.  For endless generations our forebears have looked out on planted fields, for even the most barbarous peoples cultivate land.

The farm field exercises out of doors the same sort of deep impression as the hearth within doors.  There, without, the year's sustenance is growing and maturing before one.  Depending on no whim or pulse of trade, removed from the chances of lacking employment, the owner joys in his coming harvest, knowing it is enough.  The fields acquire a charm for him apart from any special appeal they may have for the artist.

The farmer knows what is under that sod or that ploughed land.  He has walked over it many a year.  He knows what to do to it, and knows what it will give him.  The shocks of yellowing corn are the continual witness of his industry, his sagacity, and the harmony of nature with his toil.  No wild or far-flung outlook can compare in attraction with fenced fields, which hold on every square foot the history of victory for the generations that have known how to use them.

At the top of page 23 is " A Mossy Stair."  One passes this scene on the way from Manchester to Peru.  The moss and lichen tinge the rocks with olive verdure.  The fresh waters tumble over the step-like stones.  The shadows from various waving trees play over all.  When near such a spot, besides the coolness which always comes from falling water, one feels a sense of power and plenty.

"Home, Sweet Home," at the bottom of page 24, is found in the delightful nook called Dorset Hollow. The gambrel roof, the old porch, the weather-beaten walls, tell of long adjustment to the natural world and bespeak the comforts within. Without, the green natural lawn, never mowed, but worn down by farm work, is the most pleasing possible environment of the farmhouse. There the churning and sewing are done. There the family sit under the great rock maple in the twilight. There the neighbors stop for a chat. The open ground under a tree is properly called "Robin Hood's barn," and certainly no stately or pretentious erection of human hands can rival it in beauty, restfulness, freedom, and fine air.

On the top of page 27 are the lambs in August, a picture called "The Favorite Corner." The half grown lamb is the most darling creature imaginable. More poetry has been written about lambs than anybody can ever read. A dozen lambs playing about in the home field are suggestive of every warm sentiment and every dear recollection in the age-long process of human development. Historically speaking we may fairly presume that sheep were the first animals domesticated. Certainly they are a finer farm feature than any other. Doubly good for the farmer, and trebly valuable as stimulants of the imagination and feeders of the finer rural sentiments, they are the jewelled center of any landscape. In symbolism sheep and lambs enter into religion more intimately than any other animal. Indeed, more than all others combined. As the sign of the Saviour, as the symbol of meekness and willingness to be led, as the simile under which childhood and fatherly affection are woven into parable, lambs mean more to humanity than any other living things not human.

The strange obtruseness of law and custom in our day has rendered sheep raising rare. Dogs harry the sheep, and no farmer can for a moment feel that his flock is safe unless under his eye. To the settler the lambs were necessary. The matron's spinning wheel sang and her loom clanked almost the year through, as the result of sheep raising. One of the most beautiful and attractive chapters in the Bible deals with the ideal housewife and interweaves its thought with the twisted threads of her loom. She provides wool for her household.

It was common in the old days for a small boy on the farm to have set apart for him a certain lamb whose wool would be made into a suit for him. What delight in such familiar and special ordering of life!  When the boy passed the orchard clothed in his new suit, there would be his own lamb fast growing another clip of wool for another year and another suit.  The intimacy of human life with nature was emphasized and glorified by such an ideal arrangement.  Such an intimacy tended to develop local flavor, aroma in character, and a sense of kindliness in the growing youth.

There are those students of social life who believe the specialization of society will break down, and that we shall return to the pastoral state.  A worse fate could befall society.  The change would not kill poetry nor degrade character.  It would, perhaps, favor the fruitage of many valuable traits now stunted.  It would certainly take something out of the fret of our days and give room for a truer valuation of life.  The meaning of existence may easily be hidden by the multiplicity of objects and motives in modern society.  The more complex life becomes the more unstable and the less beautiful it is.  A child and a lamb and a wisp of grass; an orchard bough and the sunlight; the robin's song; a mother smiling from the door — these are the things that reach the whole of simple, deep human nature and perhaps all of the nature of God.  We are not fearful of the future of our race while love of these things lies back of our society.  We may, perhaps we ought, perchance we must, return to such loves — near to the breast of the kindly earth.  These are the loves without fever which result in no regret, which open the mind without guile.

On page 28, at the bottom, is an active haying scene.  In all the New England states hay is an important crop, but in Vermont it ranks as a chief product.  Converted into butter, cheese, and meat for market, it brings her much revenue.

The beauty of the waving fields of grass in flower is scarcely surpassed by any other natural scene.  And to be best for the herd and sweetest to its taste it must be cut in the flower.  The old method was to start into a field a crew of men, the leader of whom set the pace for the others.  The

swing of the scythe in heavy grass tested the muscle and skill of the best man, especially after the first hour. At the end of the swath all stopped to whet their scythes with the long narrow stone carried in a pocket made for the purpose in the blue overalls. The only other garment worn was a shirt, and sometimes even that was discarded. The ability of a youth to keep up with the good mower in the field was the final badge of manhood. Sometimes an old man who looked incapable of much exertion would, after the first swath, set a killing pace. His knack for mowing, as well as main strength would return to him, and he would show " the boys " how it was done.

The less sturdy or less skilful were obliged to narrow the swath in order to keep up with him. It was a disgrace to keep the pace down. The practised eye of the mower quickly took in the breadth and the smoothness of the cut. A good man was known by the path he left behind him. In this rigorous but just school there could be no pretence. Power and skill won. It was a school for character. The dissipated might start in bravely, but as the sun waxed hotter and the levelled spears of grass lay behind him, any looseness of life would tell in the stroke. Dutch courage had no place.

As the hours went on a boy would come over from the house with a miniature wooden barrel carried by a strap slung over his shoulder. The contents of this country canteen had possibly best be left by us without investigation. But human curiosity is a persistent quality. In the earliest time very strong waters were working under the wood. It was thought men could neither mow well in the field nor fight well on a man-of-war without rum. In later times the cider of the previous season was used. It had plenty of tang. It was to the American farmer what wine is to the Frenchman. After the great wave of temperance reform a mixture of sugar and ginger in water was the usual beverage. This is what the writer remembers in his childhood, but with no particular sense of longing. It was no nectar of the gods.

The mowing was done early in the day before the full power of the sun asserted itself. Six o'clock saw the crew bending their backs to the sweep of the scythe. An important reason for such early labor was that the sun might get as long a time as possible for turning the grass into hay. Somewhat late grass, not too heavy, could on very clear hot days be cured and in the barn the day it was cut. Usually it must be raked into windrows and heaped into neat cocks at night, during which time it heated somewhat. Opened the following morning and shaken out, it was ready that day for storage.

The great and looming danger was from rain. The crop was sometimes steeped when nearly dry by a heavy shower, and a great part of its value destroyed. The weather-wise person was always in demand. Everyone in the field was ready to forecast the day's sky-changes, and some, as usual, were wise and some were foolish.

The bright, faintly green, fragrant hay in the great mow was a sight to gladden man and beast. As it was thrown down at feeding time and scattered before the eager cattle it helped to compose a picturesque scene, often neglectd by the artist. The height of the mow was carefully watched by the farmer as the season advanced. By the quantity of hay on hand he regulated his purchases or sales of stock, and sometimes he sold or bought hay. In the corners by the posts or in odd nooks the hens would steal their nests. The farmer's boy was supposed to search carefully over the surface of the mows. He was sometimes rewarded by a good nestful of eggs. The hens got no small part of their rations from the grass seeds that sifted from the day's feeding of the cattle.

In " Better than Mowing," on page 222, we see an alleged farmer, in the fair valley of the Battenkill, resting his back by tickling the backs of the fishes.

In " Fording the Upper Connecticut," page 143, we see the great load being drawn homeward.

The modern haying methods have changed, but a strong back is still essential for harvesting a hay crop. The racking motion of the mowing-machine seat is stimulating to the circulation. Ordinarily no more practical method on the farm of average size, except sheer lifting, is available

for loading the hay. The pitcher sets his fork in deeply and swings to the load a weighty mass. The breaking of a fork handle is not unusual, and the pitcher is not half ashamed of such an event. A good man and a good fork, however, last long. The supple ash bears a shrewd spring, and an experienced pitcher knows how to make the handle a lasting and effectual extension of his good right arm.

The hay pressers who travel over a country where hay is sold conduct a picturesque labor. The hay is thrown rapidly into the form made to receive it, and was formerly compressed by horse power into bales held together by wooden hoops.

The marketing of loose hay was a few years since also a pleasant sight. Some of the simpler days of great cities was marked by that proceeding, as the names of sections show, Haymarket Square in Boston being a case in evidence. In those days the oxen or horses drew to town a large load very carefully trimmed to workman-like proportions. A buyer was awaited, and the wits of buyer and seller were pitted till a bargain was struck. Meantime the beasts had their fodder, and the farmer his snack of hard molasses gingerbread. On the homeward journey he carried on the bottom of his now empty rack any supplies necessary: a barrel of flour, a jug of molasses, a dried codfish, or a stick of smoked herring. Perhaps, if matters were going well with him, gingham for a gown was added to his store, and he was hardly at peace with the world until he heard his wife's comment on the figure of the goods.

The boy sometimes went up to town with the farmer, perched high on the load, on his way to the academy, and the price of the hay was passed by the calloused hand of the father to the equally calloused hand of the boy.

Anybody who wanted work on a farm carried his recommendation in his palm. No farmer would hire delicate hands to work for him. It was a wonderful life, but some weakened.

The old stage coach shown in " An Eventful Journey," on page 35, brings back an important feature of the bygone time.

We remember a thirty mile journey on such a vehicle through the country from a small city to a large village, in the hot summer time.  There were many stations where we left and took mail bags, almost invariably at a village store where everything was sold.  While the American stage coach never came up with echoing horn, the smartness and the éclat of the English coach, it was nevertheless an arrival of no small import, especially, as was often the case, when it ran only two or three times a week.

On such a journey, in the forties and fifties, and even a score of years later, the pretty city cousin would go on a visit to her country cousin, and if a youngster of an impressionable age — anything below four-score years — was also a passenger with nothing to do but to look and listen, he perhaps found himself at the day's end minus a heart and plus a responsibility for life.  The back seat of a stage coach was not the worst place for a flirtation more or less serious.  The lurch of the vehicle around corners caused some natural stir within the coach which resulted in breaking the ice of reserve.  Conversation naturally followed.  The young lady might refer to certain books, of which she knew very little, and the youth might respond by assents about books of which he knew nothing at all.  For it was a trifle of a disgrace in those days for a young man to know a novel.

Sometimes the stage moving through a back country paused long enough for the collection of a hatful of apples, picked from the roadside where they had dropped by the wall.  Sometimes a maiden would step lightly from the coach and gather the flowers by the way.  On the crests of fair hills the passengers would look out on an unaccustomed country rolling beneath them, with its streams, forests, and fields.  The corn, luscious green, to be eaten for dinner at the inn; the sheep herded in the green pastures; the white clouds sailing in the sky; the farms, and their invitation to a possible purchaser by the sign, " For Sale " — all occupied the passenger's time as fully as the prayer meeting did at home.  And to think that a little gasoline wagon has succeeded this stage-coach poetry!

## XXXV. AS IN A WINDOW

THE picture called "As in a Window," on page 39, suggests a little essay on what makes a picture beautiful or appealing. While we cannot always say why one thing is beautiful and another is ugly, we can sometimes find probable reasons for aesthetic appeals.

A necessary feature of a perfect landscape would seem to be such a contour as would lead the eye from the viewpoint to a distance — as if the soul of beauty demanded to be carried on from the present situation to one beyond. If this is true then there is something deeper in aesthetics than perfection of form and color. In them is inherent the thought that all good things lead to better things. If the object that leads the eye away is not a stream, it may be a road, a path, or a long valley. On the contrary, a certain house may be so located as to look across a valley at a range of hills standing like a wall and cutting off further vision. There is very little of appeal in such a prospect. There may indeed be a challenge to the imagination to picture what is beyond that wall. But it is openings and not barriers that stir the beholder most deeply. Thus the quaint old engraving, "The Voyage of Life," was very popular as depicting an advance. Probably Bunyan's idea in picturing by allegory life as a pilgrimage had much to do with the popularity of his *Pilgrim's Progress*. The pilgrims to the shrine at Canterbury were much impressed we are told by the beautiful approach to the high altar of the cathedral. As if it were a way to heaven, it elevated their thoughts and led them on to higher things.

It may, therefore, be laid down as the primary and possibly invariable principle of landscape beauty, that the suggestion of an opening possible for the beholder to follow, is the proper center of a picture. If here and there, as in the case of Ruskin's famous drawing of a thorn tree a portrait is secured, there is indeed an interest, but it is the same interest that centers on a piece of embroidery. It is special, not universal. It is without the best element of beauty.

When the scene has in the foreground some human feature like Constable's " Hay Wain," we are perhaps satisfied by a foreground, because in it there is so much that is sweet and homely. But even in such cases a sky beyond attracts and there is seldom a picture in which a vista is not better than a merely immediate view.

In a way this is astonishing, because, as a second element of attractive pictorial work the foreground must not only be interesting but must absorb most of the interest. The perfect picture, therefore, begins well and ends well. Attending to distance only, is not enough. One may say, apparently in a paradox, that the distance is uninteresting without a foreground. " The call of the road " begins where we are and goes on.

There is, however, another deeper and commonly recognized law: no one sees anything in a picture except what is in one's self. This is why the unfamiliar is less interesting than the familiar. People care far less for pictures of distant and exotic scenes than for those near at hand. We have reference to the vast majority. In a university town classical pictures are popular because the minds of the people have been turned toward classical things. Portraiture is always popular because we know, or think we know, more about people than about things.

A picture also has more appeal if it speaks to experience or leads the beholder to interpret. If we see a shady lane pictured we are called to its coolness. If the ocean surges are depicted we wish to bathe in them, or, if they are too fierce, the masculine impulse rises to fight them. That is why marine pictures are seldom liked by women.

Likewise pictures showing action are not liked when one is weary. Masterful pictures require beholders in a masterful mood.

Sentiment in pictures is carefully portrayed by the Dutch painters. Their domestic scenes are ever appealing. Even their drinking scenes won approval from the almost universally drinking public. The appeal to the sense of precision, of truth, of fidelity, in representation also meets a response in minds who love excellence. It is because there is a lack of regard for truth that the present shameless fad for cubism can exist. No one can love it who loves careful work — not patch work. If nature is said to be a

cubist in her broken crag formations, that is because she has not finished her work. Give her time and her landscapes gain the touch of perfection.

A sense of contrast, also, often exercises a potent charm in a picture. Thus a lovely flower growing out of a rock tends to rouse the incipient capacity for comparison. Contrast is only one aspect of comparison — the most striking aspect. That is, it shows the greatest degree of unlikeness, and therefore arrests attention. If a dark pine tree is outlined against an azure sky it succeeds in calling attention, which is the first step toward making a student. Some painters are very careful to avoid contrasts. They are of a quiet nature themselves and do not recognize the interest that contrast may have for persons of a contrary temperament. But a certain degree of contrast is necessary to any outlines at all, either in life or art. It is only a question of how violent the contrast should be. We can seldom hope to find agreement on matters of taste. It is by divergences and clashes of opinion that the various aspects of truth or beauty are set forth, and so the world gains.

The moralizing stirred by pictures is an element of interest. There is endless and silly ridicule of moralizing. The reason lies not in dislike of it, but in the fact that we all like it so well we cannot bear to indulge it in others. Everybody is moralizing all the time when he is normal, and most of the time when he is abnormal. The entire natural world being an endless storehouse of symbols, we are reminded by what we see of what we cannot see. Philosophical and religious language grew up out of the common visions and common words of the race. Thus "spirit" comes from a Latin word which means "to blow," or the "wind."

Any painting, therefore, which suggests images of things not seen at once doubles its interest. More than that, the conceit of the beholder that he is seeing deeper into the subject redounds in his mind to the benefit of the painting itself. So, as many things are seen in Browning which Browning did not see himself, many may see in a picture what the painter did not see. But if the beholder thinks the painter saw it, the pleasure in the picture is enhanced. The artist is not at hand; others interpret for him without interruption. That is their pleasure and privilege.

So far has the habit of seeing an occult, or second meaning, in pictures and in life in general been carried, that a school in philosophy has arisen to maintain that the second meaning is the more important, and the meaning for which the work or the life exists.

The comical tendency to see the face of a man or the shape of a beast in some natural feature like a tree or a cliff arises out of a subconscious tendency, old as the race, to look beyond and behind things for the message which is always being sought from the infinite.

But who has ever explained satisfactorily the artistic revulsion from new things?  In any landscape we demand the quality of mellowness.  Why is it that the most surperb edifice is uninteresting, artistically, in comparison with an old edifice?  The spick-and-span have no attraction.  Is it the deep-down natural quest for the assistance of nature in our work?  Is it the desire to gain dignity through age?  Is it that precise order and newness are unnatural and so offensive?  Frankly it is hard to say.  But it is certain that an old cottage under whose shingles the vine has penetrated so as to admit decay and cold is interesting artistically while a new cottage is not.

But the work of nature seldom looks new.  She shows her hand rarely in floods and earthquakes and scars the earth by them.  As a practice she endows every inert thing with softness and the suggestion of age.  Growths themselves springing so naturally out of what has been, do not suggest newness; only freshness and beauty.

Inevitably all men are antiquarians.  True, some are more so than others. But the charm of the past has a place in every normal mind.  This appears not only in art, but in laws that no longer have any use, and in the natural caution of our old race not to take on something we have got along pretty well without.  Possibly our sense of the solidarity of nature, and of the universal and timeless relations of life that is, and with life that was and shall be, are reflected in our shrinking from and our depictions of anything that has not borne the test of time.

But the final word about any art must be the admission of the mystery in which it is enshrouded.  We may try to explain it that effort may be a

mark of growth, of a rising power in the mind to grasp the meaning of life. But there is charm in mystery. The most fascinating aspects of art are those which we cannot explain. There is more in art, because it is a part of life, than we can ever hope to understand. It is ever a picture of reality, and as it goes on its groping way it may rise to new understandings.

Meantime we may joy in the sunset because it holds more than we understand; thus we may feel enriched that the universal mind of which we are a part is inexhaustible; that it has new beauties to be observed, new meanings to be discovered, new powers for us to wield. And these are new only as discoveries are new. They existed before we did. We are new to them; and the pleasure of living arises from relating ourselves at as many points as possible with the timeless things. Thus, "art is long and time is fleeting."

There would be no glory in the autumn scene we look at if in it we were beholding the last autumn. We know that all the color we see has been preserved and will be preserved by the alchemy of nature. The spring is the opening of an eternal succession, even as the ancient allegory of the Greeks saw it.

## XXXVI.  SUGGESTED  PROTECTION  AS  A QUALITY  IN  PICTURES

AT the bottom of page 66 is a peep through trees on the Winooski, near Montpelier. The sense of a protection in overarching trees is doubtless the secret of much of their charm. One dreams of sitting under the boughs by this fair shore, and, safe one's self, looking out at the glory beyond. Thus tree branches, which doubtless formed the first roof for man, have never lost their charm for him. They form beneath their growth his natural home.

So much of the history of our race, even to the present time, has been occupied with defending life that whatever savors of protection has its appeal to us. It is in our blood, like the huntsman's love of game-seeking, which is so rooted in many men that they annually return to it.

Anything that forms a bower, therefore, like the birches on page 60, appeals to the home-seeking instinct, and it is surprising when the tally of all the pictures we love has been made, how many depict some defensive or protective feature. One has only to run through the pages of this book to find that the pictures he likes best are marked by such features.

## XXXVII. THE LOVE OF FOUNTAINS

ONE would like to see collected all the literature connected with fountains. In the Orient, where water is scarce, at least in the classic Orient, fountains play a large part in the poetry of life as well as in its practical side.

The source of the brook, as that on page 83, where a forest fountain pours out its waters, never loses its fascination. The most impressive natural scene the writer remembers was the great gushing up from almost level ground of the springs in Florida which form a river at the fountain itself. The ancients built altars, as to a god, at the remarkable springs of the Jordan which well out from a mountain side in sudden profusion. It was not the only instance. The bubbling spring in the grassy meadow always had its almost icy cool water, so sought in haying time. Even modern science has failed to account for the great springs of Florida. It is no marvel that to the ancients springs were wholly mysterious. Yet their mystery was not fearful, but beneficent. Apparently the deity who controlled the water wished well to his worshippers. Purity and constancy and plenty were among his attributes. Health sat at the margin of the pool, and verdure drank in life there. Fountains were not only temple sites, but springs of the Muses.

## XXXVIII.  GOOD THINGS PREPARED

ON page 91 is a little old abandoned cottage among the apple trees. It is an ideal site for a homestead. Why was it ever abandoned? The Yankee has not the Celtic love for his home acres. The Teutonic people ever had roving feet. Yet here in this joyous nest between apple boughs, in rich luscious grass, in near view of noble hills, by a streamside, in a fertile valley, not far from a market town, is this abandoned paradise. The Bible represents our first parents as driven out from bliss. Their descendents have been worse than they. For we have not known enough to abide in paradise when she cradled us and crooned to us, and spread her enchantments about us. Wherever they have wandered, who were born in this forsaken home, they have reached nothing as beautiful, nothing better capable of nourishing a full and sweet life. Sometime some gifted soul will tell the story of this dumb house, and unfold the procession of history in which the edifice has had part.

Men go into forbidding regions where nature is grudging, where the endless dry prairies stretch their monotonous lengths before one. Without timber, without stone, surrounded by weed the only material for their architecture, they found new homes, afar from what they love and know. They live in naturally treeless regions, without variety, without any known history, without the benefits of an old society. And then they call their existence life. There is more of sentiment, of beauty, of profit even, in the old home acre than in the new. The soft pines call them back, the brook complains of their absence.

We must presume that men know what they seek in life, and therefore that the location of their homes is a deliberate choice. To be sure most men must live where they can thrive. But back of all this is the possibility, nay even probability that vast numbers of men are deceived as to what furnishes the better things of life. It is conceivable that some men may dwell, and cause their wives to dwell, in tawdry or dreary surroundings owing to the hope of greater gain. But such persons are gaining only a little bit of the world and losing their own souls.   Is not the first question for a young husband and wife, where can we rear healthy children, and surround them so that they may grow in the best knowledge?

The fact that millions of children are growing up in filthy city streets, dodging, sometimes successfully, the motor truck, is proof that millions are careless of their offspring.   Such parents plainly say, " We love other things better than our children's welfare."   The person who chooses four rooms on a third floor for his family rather than a cottage outlook such as is shown either on page 91 or page 92 is either of low mentality or low morality.   One who prefers to walk home after work through filth, and between hot walls rather than on such roads as fork on page 103 may think he is sane, but is he?   If he prefers to gaze on a blank wall rather than on a river valley such as page 108 shows there is something wrong with him. Whatever it is it is costing him too much to live as he lives.

## XXXIX.   PICTURES OF FLOWERS

WE have lately noted a revival of the fashion which placed pictures of flowers in dining rooms.   It is a good sign of an increasing love of flowers.   Masses of fine color such as pictures of that sort furnish are the next best thing to the flowers themselves.   For the pictures provide constant and unfading beauty.

Floral wall papers have long been in fashion — too long.   The repetition on a wall of hundreds of identical floral decorations is enough to madden anybody, not to confine our thought to artists.   It is far better, if the wall is such that it must be covered, to paint it or to paper it in a neutral tint and then to place floral groups here and there like panels. Thus a repetition of the same thing is avoided, and one is induced to attend to the particular beauty of one group after another.

This subject might be enlarged profitably by a consideration of wall papers in general, did space serve.   At least let us say, let no fad be followed,

merely because it is a fad. The reason often given for covering walls with paper is that it is desired to make the home cheerful! Any normal mind is effected by the result with anything but cheerfulness. Or, one will say, "We have put old fashioned papers on our walls," with the emphasis on the "old."

In the present return to many of the tastes and customs of our ancestors the superficial person has often missed the point entirely. For the sane, the praiseworthy fashion is of course to return to the old fashion merely as it had charm, or merit, or any thing worthy in it. For nothing is good merely for its age. We have heard of two or three instances where plumbing was omitted from old or restored old houses, because "They did not have plumbing in those days!"

Unless the fashion of reviving the past is to be marked with some discrimination it will soon lose credit, and will deserve to do so.

There are, let us be frank, many old customs which we cannot too soon, or too completely forget. The charm and worth of modern life will consist in the discrimination with which it selects the best of the past and incorporates it in the present.

Some raise the question whether incongruity and bad taste may not result from such a selection. The incongruity and bad taste consists in mixing various forms of architecture or alleged architecture, in one building, and placing in one room, furniture of several periods or of no period at all.

A consistent old fashioned interior is easily attained without the inconveniences of the past, and without adopting all the old-time decoration. For a wall covered with wood is a still older form of finish than a wall covered with paper. At best paper is a poor and mean makeshift, and when first used it frankly admitted itself to be a substitution for something better. This appears in the panels in wall papers of the earliest sort, in which wooden panels are imitated. Of course the landscape paper, as it cannot too often be said, was for the use of persons who could not afford pictures. So far is that fact forgotten, that pictures are very generally seen placed over figured wall paper — a practice in very bad taste, unless the figures are small and unobtrusive in color. The obvious reason for hanging a picture is to afford pleasure or instruction, or both. So pictures are hung — and sometimes executed — by every household.

But the eye is confused by mixed colors surrounding a picture, and still more is it confused if picture is overlaid on picture. The excellent reason for surrounding water colors with wide, quiet margins is to enhance the effect of the water colors. The first object, therefore of a housewife in Vermont or elsewhere, is to avoid multiplicity of details on any wall, or indeed anywhere in or around her home.

The call of good taste is for emphasis on something good and worth while. Therefore we must have fewer and better objects on our walls and our floors. Overloaded horses have a redress, sometimes, in a society organized to protect them. Overloaded houses have no legal means of relief. We remember one parlor wall — and it was one of the most beautiful wainscot walls in America — on which, on one side of a room, over fifty objects were hung, drawn, or quartered. The effect was distressing, but not to the owner, who had indulged what she spoke of as her own taste. In the same room, on another wall, was one very large and exquisite family portrait done by a master. Here the owner had before her eyes continually a good and a bad, and she was the author of the bad and liked it. Is it remarkable that some despair of educating the people in good taste? In the instance quoted — in respect to culture far from a probable reader of this book — the family was old and distinguished. They had thought it worth while to be educated in everything good, except in those things always nearest and most obvious — their walls and their furniture.

Good pictures are expensive, it is said, and therefore the advice given above is impracticable to most people. No; steel engravings and many other good engravings are very inexpensive. Even water colors in good taste, if confined, we will say, to floral representations need not be expensive. Many housewives have themselves decorated their walls very prettily and without offending persons of fastidious taste.

Sometimes wall papers are encouraged on the score of their cleanliness.

But a painted wall surpasses them in this respect. Wall paper to be kept fresh must be renewed. A painted wall of plaster or of wood, whether painted or not, may be washed whenever the housewife desires. And if it is not washed for years it is yet more cleanly and more sanitary than wall paper. Still, the objection to wall paper is mostly overcome if plain paper, or paper scarce removed from plainness, is used. Then a few pictures, wall cupboards, or boxes; an old chart or map, an early print, may serve to give interest and dignity and warmth to a house.

## XL. GARDEN ARRANGEMENT

IN a book dealing mostly with rural life some attention should properly be paid to gardens.

The first principle of the lady of the house in Vermont, must often be conservation of time. For this reason she should choose for the most part for her garden those flowers which renew themselves annually, and those flowers which are hardy enough to survive severe winters. Thus her labors will be lightened; for it will be noticed we are presuming, as it is safe to do, that most of the flower garden labors fall to women. Men are not persuaded unless they are florists, that a flower garden is important. The exceptions to this statement lament the rule.

In the arrangement of a garden the path — there is generally but one — is the natural focus. On its borders may be grouped rows of small flowers, to be followed in their rear by others of higher growth so that one row may offset or reinforce another. In a little house-garden any effort at landscape effects is unnecessary. Formality may be encouraged in a small garden, though, to us at least, it becomes a bore in a large garden. If instead of a grouping of all the flowers together one chooses to cultivate clumps of flowers against old boulders, or along fence rows, the result is often more pleasing. Such an arrangement tends to enlarge the general aspect of beauty about a home.

" Old fashioned flowers " is an amusing term. Of course we understand what it means. But fortunately He who makes flowers grow does not distinguish between old and new. There is an eternity in every flower however ephemeral its bloom may be.

That thought brings to our mind another: that those flowers are to be preferred which have a long blooming season. Carelessness about choice may result in a dull garden during most of the summer. Cosmos is deservedly popular because its gay and abundant bloom extends away beyond any ordinary early frost, and by a little protection it may even go on to very severe frost. Thus one should choose some of the first flowers that bloom, like the crocuses, and by judicious selection make the whole summer bright. If a quarter of the garden blooms at once, and the bloom is somewhat distributed, an ample array of blossoms is provided, for solid color or universal colors in a garden are as much to be avoided as elsewhere.

It has been said, perhaps by wise men, that nervous or lonely women have their balance and serenity restored by garden attendance. Where is the mother or the daughter of the house more beautiful than among her flowers, herself the most beaming and attractive of them all?

There are some women who can hardly be content without flowers the year through. For such there is joy in life, and a fullness that cannot otherwise come into the heart.

In a cold climate like Vermont a garden is especially valued. Flowers are loved there more than in regions where they flourish most of the year. The garden is eagerly thought of in the late spring, and is a delight all the greater because it is long in coming.

## XLI. A VISIT TO MT. MANSFIELD

WE made the ascent of Mt. Mansfield some years ago before the advent of the motor car. The kind people of St. Johnsbury had told us we must go to Stowe and there we would find the wagons to take us up the mountain. We imagined that Stowe lay snuggled at its base, and that mountain guides and wagons could be had in plenty. But reality often differs from pictures in the brain. After a rattling ride from Morrisville in a well-filled wagonette we drew up before the inn door in Stowe only to receive the inhospitable information, " All wagons for the day left for Mt. Mansfield an hour ago." And Mt. Mansfield itself, instead of hanging in a protecting, fatherly fashion about the village farms, lay placidly off in the distance, five miles, they said, like a giant asleep on his back. In fact there is so much resemblance between the outline of the mountain and a prostrate human figure, especially the face, that prominent parts of the mountain have been named The Forehead, The Nose, The Chin.

How to reach this sleeping giant we did not know, unless we walked. As our time was limited it was not wise to spend the night at the inn and wait for a wagon next day. But if we walked to the foot of the mountain, we felt we would be too tired for the four hours' climb necessary to reach the summit. When our gloom was darkest the proverbial ray of light appeared in the shape of a blue-coated man, who, for a good round sum, offered to drive us to the mountain and there leave us to find our way to the top by following the wagon road.

We were hungry, but there was no time for dinner. We must be on our way at once, we were told, or darkness would overtake us on the steep mountain side. We looked off to the land of our journey and found it thickly wooded. Lost in the mountains among the tall trees not seeming an agreeable fate, we hastily purchased bananas, sweet chocolate, and crackers, climbed into the carry-all which our blue-coated friend had provided, and made a brisk dash toward the wooded height.

NOTE. The accompanying sketch is written by an admirer of Vermont who signs the initial "H."
THE AUTHOR

At the last house at the foot of the mountain we left our luggage to be picked up by the man who carried the express to the summit. Then gaily bidding adieu to our driver, we tied our sweaters about our waists, picked up some suitable sticks, entered the wooded road, and began our climb.

The first thing we noticed was that it was hot; the next, that we could see nothing of the wonderful views we had expected. Up, up, we went, but the encircling trees hid the landscape. The road was rough, and we soon tired. Should we ever reach the top? Nature was kind, however, and at climbing intervals of about twenty minutes provided us with a spring. Here we would halt — drop down in fact — eat of our hastily collected food-store, drink the cool water, bathe our faces in it, and wonder what next. So the afternoon wore away, and feeling more and more the strain on our muscles and the weariness of exertion, we thought only of the hours of rest which should be ours when the hotel at the top of the mountain was reached.

But suddenly we came out of the woods, and the view burst upon us! Green sunny peaks were everywhere; beautiful clouds were filling, spreading, then filling again and floating majestically aloft; while away in the distance loomed the Presidential Range — Mt. Washington, Mt. Adams, Mt. Jefferson, Mt. Madison — among the White Hills of New Hampshire! All thoughts of rest vanished, all weariness oozed away, and filled with exhilaration excited by the beauty of the scene and the patriotic appeal of mountain names and pride of belonging to a country so grand, we rushed to the simple hostelry which stood among the rocks, secured a room for the night and went forth to explore.

Never had we thought the old giant lying on his back, as we had seen him from the valley of Stowe, could have so much beauty in store for us! We walked on and on for miles. We perched on crags, we wandered over crooked footpaths and crouched in terror at strange booming noises. As the region was totally unknown to us, we wondered if wild beasts lurked behind the rocks, and what made the low-growing hemlocks wave with so much agitation. We peered about cautiously, looking for shining eyes

among the shrubs; we listened again, and the boom! boom! sounded more ominous than ever. But no wild animal came from a secret hiding place; no lions or tigers sprung across our path. Then it was we discovered the top of the mountain was full of caves, and that the wind clutching at their dark throats, and roaring pitiless threats into their unimpressive ears, was responsible for our fright.

But it was after our late dinner that the true magnificence of the scene came to us and we felt fully repaid for our long climb of several hours before. Mt. Mansfield is more than four thousand feet high, and one of its highest points, called The Nose, is not far from The Summit House. Just as the sun was making his adieux to the western world, we climbed the crags that make The Nose and watched the panorama before us. Miles away, but seemingly close at our feet, lay Lake Champlain, pulsing with rosy lights, and beyond were the Adirondacks, range on range, beckoning to the almost illimitable stretches that lay between us and the Golden Gate of our Pacific shores. Wondrous clouds floated, like Islands of the Blessed, in a sea of opalescent tints. To float with them into Eternal Peace seemed easy and natural. The long sigh which came with the purple twilight was a high tribute to the beauty we had seen. When we closed our eyes to sleep that night it was with the thought that our cup was really too full, for we should see the sun rise in the morning!

But alas-and-alack-a-day! The sun never rose at all! As if Nature felt she had allowed us enough pleasure for one visit she drew a cloud of mist over the whole mountain. When we awoke a drizzling rain was falling, and not an object was visible twenty feet from the hotel door. No wagons would venture up or down the mountain on a day like this. The thermometer had fallen to forty degrees, men and women shivered in what wraps they could furnish and huddled disconsolately about a little iron stove in the plain living room. We were marooned on the mountain for an indefinite period. Then it was that man turned to contemplate his brother, and blotted-out crag and sky were forgotten in tales of human interest.

The night before at our table had sat a man of waxen complexion who had given not a glance at the excellent dinner which was being served, but had asked the waiter for a quart of hot milk. A quart of hot milk on the top of Mt. Mansfield! Now it seems that the milk supply of the hotel came mainly from one cow, which browsed among the low bushes and made pleasant echoes among the rocks as the tongue of her metallic bell swung heavily while she snatched her scanty sustenance. A quart of milk to one man! At that rate how could each guest be properly supplied? The waiter stood aghast, but the gourmand took a small cake of uncooked, compressed cereals from his pocket and assured his provider that that was all he would have to eat unless the milk was forth coming. Doctor's orders! Forth came the milk. And now on this misty day, when it was impossible to leave the hotel as he had expected, the cakes of grain had given out and the cow was lost in the fog. Poor man! We listened with sympathy to his accounts of doctor's orders and to the tale of a gain of twenty pounds in two months on the diet prescribed, but secretly we were pleased to see him obliged to eat chicken at the mid-day meal, and no doubt secretly he was pleased himself to think the hardships of travel had reduced him to such straits!

The man and his party were planning to visit Smuggler's Notch, not many miles away, as soon as the sun shone again. Here we were told the cliffs rose one thousand feet and had looked down on many a deed of darkness and daring. For during the War of 1812 with England, and the days of the Embargo Act which preceded it, some Vermonters took the law into their own hands and traded with Canada as they saw fit. Their boats came down Lake Champlain, ran up the entering rivers sometimes, unloaded their goods, and then other smugglers took the merchandise across the country. Vermont was very sparsely settled at that time, and party feeling in opposition to the war ran high. In fact all New England opposed the war as contrary to its commercial interests, but Vermont was better situated for romantic deeds than some parts of the country. Someone spoke of the famous Black Snake, the smuggling boat that was finally

captured up the Winooski; someone spoke of cattle thieves and their adventures with the officers of the law; someone spoke of Vermont's heroes in the war and all agreed that these far outnumbered the few lawless citizens who had plotted and planned in Smuggler's Notch.

All the time we were talking a grave looking man with fine features sat silently by himself in a corner and seemed not to hear a word. Rumor said he was a famous judge who seldom spoke outside the courtroom. He made yearly visits to the little hostelry on the top of Mt. Mansfield and seemed to be content with the beauty of the views and in no need of human society. Day wore on into evening. Card tables were brought out and some forgot the cold and dreariness of their surroundings in watching for kings, queens, and aces. Some continued to talk, but the silent man did not notice. We passed him with a bit of awe as we said goodnight to the company and mounted the stairs to our sleeping quarters. Though speech is silvern, silence is often golden, and we wondered if we had not erred in our much talking with strangers. But the time would have passed drearily indeed had nobody said anything.

The next morning seeming as gray as the day before we resolved not to get up at all but to ward off the chill by staying in bed. Disconsolately we turned our faces into our pillows and tried to sleep, only to be soon roused by a shouting, a commotion, and a quick awakening to the fact that we had surrendered too soon to despair. The storm was over, the sun shining, and the world once more was ours! A glance from our window showed the glory and grandeur of the mountain scenery in even more loveliness than before. Fellow tourists were shouting excitedly to us from the rocks below; the hemlocks were glistening in the clear light; the cowbell was tinkling cheerfully near at hand. With all haste we rushed into the out-of-doors and hurried to a point of vantage.

The clouds that had settled on us the day before, drenching us with mist, were now lying below us a half mile down the mountain side. As we looked they began to break, and lift, and float out over the world at our feet. To one who had never seen this phenomenon before, as we had not, the sight was thrilling and inspiring.  Like wraiths the mists curled and gathered in the hollows, then floated off towards the sun as if to offer praise.    Sometimes they collected in large masses and spread out for miles, then rose and broke again as though ashamed of the selfishness that would hide from us the beautiful landscape.   So gathering, rising, breaking, floating off into the blue, the cloud fairies held us entranced until at last all disappeared and left us so full of joy at the loveliness of our surroundings that we rebelled strongly at the thought of leaving it, as we knew we must.   As a last goodby we wandered once more among the windhaunted caves and listened to their booming music; once more we followed winding paths and discovered objects we had missed before; once more we climbed The Nose and looked out toward Champlain; once more we turned towards Smuggler's Notch and its romantic haunts.   Our two days had been full of interest.   Should we ever come again to this spot? We would be foolish or most unfortunate did we not; and next time we would plan to spend weeks instead of days in the region.

So great was the hold of the mountain upon us that when we left that afternoon we walked the first two miles of the downward road and allowed the stage to overtake us.   By doing this we could pause when a break in the trees gave us a bit of rapture, or when something interesting caught our attention.   We could examine the stones and mosses, pick the occasional flower and fill our lungs at will with the purest of pure air.   There was no apprehension in this downward journey, as there had been in our ascent. We were carrying back with us the memory of broad views and grand summits, and we were happy.

## XLII.  OLD  NEW  ENGLAND  HOMES

A SMALL work with the above title was prepared by the author, designed for rich illustration in color.   But after about a dozen copies had been issued it was thought best to withdraw it from the market and

to publish certain of its contents in this more popular form. The text of this earlier work is used through the title "The Time of Day."

## THE HEARTH

Since men discovered how to make a fire the hearth has been the center of their lives. Every human generation except one has sat about the hearth at evening. The last generation "escaped" it — a doubtful mark of progress. Our ancestors got their food, warmth and light from the hearth. Hundreds of our lineal ancestors crawled before an open fire, and after the mother's breast that fire was their first mystery. It taught their first lesson in self restraint. Their gaze from the day that they first "took notice" till they were bent and senile was for some part of every day into the fascinating, soothing, alluring glow of the fireplace. Humanity was born close by the fire, and passed away from the fire into the unseen world. Love and lore began at the fireside. It was the symbol of comfort and affection and cheer. It was the spot where sacred and secular met.

Fire was a precious thing. Our own grandfathers sometimes went miles in winter, through deep snows, to "borrow fire" when they had neglected to keep their coals alive. With wet wood it was easier to borrow than to use the flint and steel. A hearth without glowing coals was the sign of desolation. The aboriginal crawling naked before the fireplace loved it no less than did the king's son.

## SAGAS OF THE FIRELIGHT

It was at evening or in bitter winter storms that the children crept between grandpa's knees and listened to the sagas of long ago, while the weird firelight played on their awestruck little faces. Before writing, history was perpetuated by stories handed down from father to son of the deeds of *their* fathers, which, we may be sure, lost nothing in the telling. Demigods got their shape by the firelight, as their great figures were outlined by the reverend grandsire, and the monstrous leaping shadows in the dark corners of the room lent reality and fascinating horror to their substantial ghosts. "Tell me a story" is the first popular demand for literature, for history if it were forthcoming, but at any rate for a story that must be told with sufficient art to seem real.

At first the grandfather, his activities circumscribed to hovering before the blaze, kept himself to the general and recent history of the family. But the tune was soon demanded with variations. Details were added to supply the demand. Alluring side paths were followed. A new adventure must be supplied to give coherence, and fill up the gaps.

Old Homer tried his tale first, we may be sure, at the fireside on his own grandsons. As his hand swept the strings and gained confidence the neighbors gathered around. That was a theatre for you! What were Mrs. Siddons and her train compared with the great black but glowing background of the stone fireplace in the ancient hall, the grand old harper, and the eager Greek faces turned toward him, while the roof returned the falling echoes of "the good old times."

Literature is the weaving of fact and imagination into a texture of beauty and coherence. What subtler stimulus of imagination than this same crinkling spark-chase over the surface of the back log and the little flames spitting from the crevasses of the fagots! Any man is a poet when he muses by the glowing hearth. Literature got its proper cantos by the fireside. The tale, for unity's sake, must reach its climax in an evening, before the bright eyes of the listeners glazed with languor, and so as the blaze died down, the story drew to an end, leaving only a suggestive question unanswered, to serve as a beginning for the next saga night.

Or it was a story of true love in distress? In the half shadow behind the narrator a strong young hand would reach out for that of a coy maid, and by the fire grew a love and loyalty reaching its fitting culmination when the youth led home the maiden to keep his hearth alight and to rear a new generation.

There was also a beginning of state-craft by the hearth. The council fires of savage and sage witnessed the gathering of chiefs and elders to form the policies of war and peace.

In later times it was the love light that suggested to invention ways of bettering the fireplace. When America was settled men built ovens in the backs of the fireplaces. In these ovens the fire which was started had no separate flues but blazed forth from the open oven doors and found its way up the great chimney. Then the ashes were cleared and the baking done in the same cavity. It was an afterthought of some good man to relieve his wife from hovering over the hot blaze on the main hearth to superintend her baking. He therefore built an oven at the side of the fireplace with a subordinate flue leading into the great chimney.

### THE HANGING OF THE CRANE

In the older American fireplaces there was no crane, but a tough pole fixed above the blaze on lugs at each side of the opening. To test the savory kettle of broth the housewife must lean over the flame. Some good man, who wished to save the fair face of his wife from this ordeal, invented a crane on which the pot could be swung out and filled, tried, or emptied at leisure. So the " hanging of the crane " came to mean the setting up of a new family.

The pot hooks were made of different lengths to bring the vessels within a proper distance of the fire. The flat shovel used in passing the mince pies and bean pots into the oven was called a slice. The warming pan was filled with coals and moved about between cold sheets for the benefit of guests or invalids, the hardy not requiring or at least not admitting the need of such artificial aids. There was attached to the ceiling a long pole or two, on which was hung the ironing to air before being stored in drawers strewn with lavender.

In my boyhood we possessed an ancient single ox-yoke, which had been used on " Old Star " (an ox so called from the white spot on his forehead) to drag into the kitchen the great back log. It was of course impossible to drive a pair of oxen through the narrow doors, but probably the neat mother thought the one great beast enough — almost a bull in a china shop! And the log was usually well coated with snow or ice!

In later times the genius of the brothers Adam in England and their grateful imitators here, made the fireplace what it deserved to be, the center of home decoration, and today as one tours through the back country one may often come upon a ruinous dwelling with a fireplace well worth negotiating for.

It was natural that the parlor fireplace should receive the best skill of the local carpenter. Above it the chimney drew in, leaving the room for cupboards where the family treasures were stored.

It was not unusual for a fireplace to be seven or eight feet broad. This generation has mistaken the meaning of " the chimney corner." It was not a corner of the room near the chimney but a side of the fireplace itself within which the grandfather sat, on those milder days when only a portion of the hearth was required for the fire. A fireplace in Warwick, Rhode Island, was so large that three sets of andirons had their place within it, in a row, and the black oak beam which formed the lintel was nineteen inches through and so hard, from generations of slow roasting, that it was impossible to drive into it the point of a knife. Many a fireplace was as high as a man's shoulder, and the stars could be seen by peering upward.

Santa Claus could easily descend such a chimney, though his proportions were as generous as the children were led to believe.

There is, could we know it, a legend and a romance connected with every old fireplace. The spot is full of sentiment and symbolism. There were other festoons than simple strings of dried apple and pumpkin hung about the wide chimney-piece. There twined the tendrils of many fond memories, and there sat the dear ghosts of other years.

In some houses there was an enlargement made in the chimney, at the second story, and a narrow door admitted to a stone floored chamber where the meats from the Christmas killing were hung to cure and smoke, and were never removed from their nails till wanted for use.

In some instances the great chimney contained secret cupboards or even stairs where the wife might hide if attacked by the Indians.

There were often, in the larger houses, seven or eight fireplaces, grouped around a single chimney, on two floors.

The more pretentious homes had more than one chimney — the regular number in a really good house of 1790 being four, two at each end built into the brick end of the house. Hence many old houses are seen with brick ends, and fronts and backs of wood. Thus a household was " between two fires " — one at each side room facing the great hall. The outsides of the rooms in the case of one chimney only, were very cold, and in bitter weather, there was a frost line on the floor, part way between the hearth and the outside wall. Whittier's " Snow Bound " gives us many details of the old life.

It was necessary to keep the cellars nearly at the point of freezing, because the year's stock of vegetables was stored there. Apples stored in a dark, cold, and somewhat damp cellar kept till spring without wilting, and the winter evenings were beguiled by a row of this unrivaled fruit toasting before the blaze, and turned by the expectant children. For their elders a jug of cider, also home made, simmered by the side of the hearth.

In the earliest days a spit for the great meat roasts was contrived, at first turned by boy-power, until an ingenious and perspiring young American arranged a dog-power and secured his liberty at the expense of his humble companion.

The bannocks were baked on a smooth sheet of iron, or even of wood, set on the hearth slantwise to the blaze. Doubtless the dreadful American appetite for hot bread descends from those days.

### OCCUPATIONS OF THE FIRESIDE

Besides the apples to watch and the cider to warm, there was corn to pop or parch. Our fathers learned from the Indians how to use parched corn. The kernels that did not pop were brayed in a mortar and carried on hunting trips. Enough for many days' supply could thus be kept at hand, superior to our breakfast foods and ready to eat at any brookside. The popped corn was a favorite dish with milk. Corn was of course as new to our ancestors as to their children. The lives of the first comers were saved by buying or borrowing from the Indians. While corn was inferior to wheat its yield per acre was greater, and it was easier to cultivate and care for, requiring no mill or tedious baking. For these reasons corn is still popular in the poorer parts of our country. The mountaineers of the Appalachians still use it in the simple manner of our ancestors. Indeed if one wishes to know how the early English settlers lived he has only to go into a mountain home, where he will find the same utensils, articles of diet, and domestic habits that marked our fathers.

The hand-loom, the flax-wheel and the wool spinning-wheel, the hand-hetchels and cards for flax and wool provided all that was required for the wear of every member of the family. The grandmother knit all the stockings, mittens, scarfs, and hoods.

The cheese press and the churn, the mortar, and often a cobbler's bench stood along the wall. If an ingenious member of the family did not make the footwear, an itinerant cobbler came as a guest until he had fitted out the family for the year.

### THE VERSATILITY OF THE SETTLER

Every farm was a factory and a university. There was nothing necessary to the comfort of human life that was not raised or made at home, except salt. Hats from their own straw; brooms from their own broom corn; and rushes for the kitchen floors, cut in their own swamp. For their woodwork, linseed oil from their own flax; to render their boots waterproof and supple, neatsfoot oil from their own cattle. Feathers from their own geese supplied soft beds and pillows necessary in the unwarmed rooms of a cold winter. Maple furniture, either the beautiful bird's-eye or the plain wood, was hard and strong, and when men required even greater strength there was oak. The supple ash made their fork and ax handles; the birch was as beautiful as mahogany, and as a wood to burn it was the perfect poetry of a blaze. If a great wall had been built around the home and acres of a pioneer, he would not have felt any lack of food or raiment.

COPYRIGHT 1903 BY WALLACE NUTTING

It was the variety of his occupations that broadened the mind of a settler. A man who can do anything is somebody, and has learned to think. A woman who has clothed and fed her own household has a strength and dignity impossible to a mere poseur. A man who can carve a forest can build a state.

The almost miraculous burst of inventive genius that appeared in America is to be traced to the putting of so many good minds to doing such varied tasks. A high class of laborers invents labor-saving devices. If modern division of labor proceeds too far it will narrow the laborer more than it will help the labor. If necessity is the mother of invention, the people who find everything supplied for them will not invent.

Our fathers digged their wells and wanted a refrigerator. One farmer made a recess half-way down in his well and there stored the summer's butter for the winter. This remarkable well is in South Woodstock, Vermont. The water in a deep well is not very much above freezing.

### PATCHWORK QUILTS

These old quilts are not merely an ornamental covering for the bed. They are also a mosaic of affection. See here a bit of calico that was in Bessie's first apron; and here is a piece of silk from grandmother's wedding gown; that is a relic of Jimmie's first pinafore; this square was from your Uncle Eli's flowered waistcoat. Handle the old quilt reverently, for every triangle in it marks the laughs or tears or prayers of another generation.

The quilting frame was sustained at the corners by chairs or tables, and the good women of the village gathered for the quilting bee. Reached out side by side over the odd patterns were the gnarled red hands of years of labor and the soft white fingers of young girlhood. The corners were cut out to fit around the big old bed-posts, and domestic art achieved its triumphs in the arrangement of the quaint pieces in attractive designs.

The fair hands of those days also wove the lovely blue-checked counterpanes which have come down to us. Some of them are now deemed worthy of the state chambers of persons high in place. Their colors were always soft and harmonious. Alas! we are in danger of losing some of the old arts as we gain new ones. I have sought long for some one skilled in drawing in the old testers that crowned the canopies of the high posters.

### THE FOOD OF THE FATHERS

This was the biggest question they had to face. They did not land in a region where nature was especially bountiful. It was an ancient joke that the seed must be shot into the ground from a gun, and the sheep's noses were sharp, working in between the rocks.

One family in New England has picked rocks for eight generations from the same farm. Literal millions of pebbles or boulders line the roadsides and field divisions. But whenever a plough cuts the sod it turns up a new rocky harvest. Many old farms raised nothing to spare but boys. The food question at once swallowed up every other.

Corn was hand-ground until a mill could be set up. The simplest and best form of corn bread was made by adding merely salt and water to the meal and spreading a very thin mixture on a board before the fire. This diet is guaranteed to cure any digestive derangement! It is almost the best food. But the corn must have all its sweetness, and the meal must be kept in very small parcels so as not to heat and lose its delicious flavor. Rye was later mixed with corn meal and the result was what I used to hear called Rhine-Injun — being, I supposed, some species of European red man. Great was my astonishment to find it spelled " rye an' Injun." This mixture was made into brown bread and baked in the big ovens to go with beans.

By a kind provision of Providence beans will grow on the poorest soil so that " bean land " is the worst name to call a field. It is a sad provincialism to suppose baked beans peculiar to New England. On the Lake of Galilee the men who row for tourists all day and for fish all night, make their meal of beans and a flapjack — the latter pulled in a roll from the pocket. Beans have been found, chemically and experimentally,

to contain more nutriment than any other form of food, being far superior to meat. Yet our fathers did not eat beans more than eight or, at most, fifteen times a week! The new beans came on Saturday night. The pot went back into the big oven so that with the bread, breakfast was piping hot Sunday morning. Many wonder how the family kept awake at church. After they had driven through the storm and took their seats in an edifice without any heat except from the pulpit, our fathers felt the need of something warming within, and beans are a steady six-hour fire, without replenishing. It is true that, in August, somnolence might mar the perfect peace of the church, but at any rate nobody was prematurely hungry for dinner. The beans came on warmed up for Monday morning and noon. As a rule the wives restricted their use to two of the daily meals, but where the boys were specially fond of beans they were sometimes allowed a few for supper and between meals. A real New Englander never tires of beans. He knows that be the cost of living what it may, the nation is safe while the bean holds out to burn. Of course, when the uninitiated eat beans and sit down at once to write poetry they may produce lame meter. They should know that milking and feeding ten cows before breakfast and similar light exercises afterwards should precede their poetic effusions. It is well known that America's great lights in poetry were reared in beandom. Without beans, no Whittier, Longfellow, Lowell, Holmes, or Emerson. Beans would be had for a French gentleman. For a New Englander, rolling logs, pulling stumps, riving boulders, and ploughing out roads and arguing on predestination, beans were the ideal diet, and nothing will be invented to displace them from supremacy. As string beans early in the season, or cranberry beans in midsummer or bean porridge in the spring — what could rival their infinite variety?

They were cooked with a piece of salt pork and required no other seasoning except vinegar from the barrel of soured cider, made from the natural fruit of the orchard.

In the autumn and winter a barrel of salt pork and another of corned beef was packed — or more if the family were large. The hams were hung in the chimney or smoke-house.   The odds and ends made mince-meat. In using all without waste, modern scientific meat-packers could teach our fathers nothing.

The doughnuts were fried either in lard or suet.   A suet pudding had honor.   Our fathers learned to use vegetables much more largely than in England.   The quick hot summers were favorable to most sorts.   A vegetable hash, with a slice of corned beef, was a dish for great men.   The dice of red beets, yellow turnips and white potatoes helped, with the bright-checkered aprons and " linsey-woolsey " about the board, to give a fine bright air of color.

The milkweed supplied unrivalled greens.   Dandelions brightened every dooryard.   The mustard grew by the back window.   In the " cut-down " (where the trees had been felled) sprang up the most luscious blackberries, raspberries, and strawberries.   An occasional bear disputed possession of these dainties, and it was found feasible at times to send a young man along with Priscilla to protect her — from the bear hugs.   She could always fill her basket first — her basket which she had made, or bartered to obtain it from an Indian.   The elderberry made a famous wine, and before tallow became plenty the bayberry supplied candles.

Fish and venison relieved the fare of sameness.   The cod was an early source of wealth, and was called the " Cape Ann Turkey."   A salt cod always hung in the cellar-way so that unexpected guests could not surprise the home without a substantial reserve.   The eloquence of New England politicians and clergymen has been traced by some to the quantities of smoked, pickled and fresh tongue which they devoured.   When we add that calves' brains also assisted — maturing by wise process of gestation in the growing boys — we may see the beginning of wisdom.

As soon as possible wheat became, as always among Aryan nations, the main reliance in breadstuffs.   The lye from wood ashes suggested a way to prepare hulled corn.

The English tart speedily gave way to pie, the mince-meat and the apples, the squash and the berries being so temptingly convenient.   Plums,

which grow to perfection in England and on our north Pacific coast, and which supply the national "sweet" of England, do not come to their finest maturity in New England.

## HOME VIRTUES

It is probably true, as a broad statement, that generations of men living in apartment houses cannot remain free. The habits of independence in thought and action which are stimulated by dwelling in a detached home are necessary to educate a free man. An apartment house, with a suite of rooms in which everything is furnished, is calculated to sap the manliness of young Americans and so far will in time come to be immoral. That is to say, if everything is furnished for a man he grows to be a parasite.

Our fathers hewed watering troughs from logs. They made buckets of wood and thus became their own coopers. They wanted a damp-proof powder carton, and found it in an ox horn, and from other horns they made their buttons, and even swore by " the great horn spoon." Few families had much china; fewer had tin. The plates were trenchers of wood turned on home lathes. Pottery though rude was serviceable. But the age was, above all others before or since, the wood age. Wood of so many good sorts was ready to their hands. There is no non-conductor better than wood. Place your hand on a log a foot away from a blaze and you find the wood barely warm. Finding colder winters here than in England, the settlers soon fenced out the winter by the lapped clapboard and the wain-scotted wall. Their vehicles, even to the axles as in the " one hoss shay," were all of wood or leather, except perhaps the tires and linch-pin.

What they could not make they did not want. They were a fine example of Socrates' half humorous, wholly wise saying, on going through the stalls of a market: "How many things there are in the world that I don't need! "

There can be no doubt that the versatility cultivated by their situation in life was the source of that contempt in our ancestors for shiftless people. As a child I remember the term shiftless used by my grandfather as an epithet of opprobrium as strong as any attaching to moral turpitude. The contrast was vast between their time and ours, when the same man who lays a brick cannot lay a tile.

The hand of our grandmother! It was worthy to be carved in marble by a master and the effigy kept under glass like the crown jewels! What of deftness and cunning and experience and strength and tenderness did it lack! Surely the hand — when it is glorified by such knowledge and use and such a spirit — is a fascinating and adorable member, worthy to be kissed, nay almost worshiped, despite its wrinkles and hardened knuckles. It founded and fed and furnished a family and a nation.

### FLOOR COVERINGS

In the ancient houses of persons in modest circumstances the rag carpet strips and the braided rugs were all that was necessary. The carpet was woven on the great loom that stood at one end of the living room. The braided rugs could be formed in so many patterns and sizes that they afforded ample variety. In the best sorts the braids ended with every revolution so as to make a complete stripe, and were not sewn spirally round and round.

When cotton was dear and silk dearer, every old bit from a garment and at last the garment itself went into the rugs. Thus each had an individuality, and the mother as she sat sewing could not cast her eyes down without being reminded of various members of her family who had once worn what was now a strand in the rug. No wonder that these rugs which wore like iron were handed down two generations and more. They wove into their quaint colors the comedy and tragedy of the family; they were a history of the old years, and meant far more than old China.

Their value and durability was greater when the braid was small and close and the edges well turned in. They were sewn tightly with strong linen threads, and it was counted as a reproach to the maker if a seam started.

The round and the oval shapes were most common. There was a bit

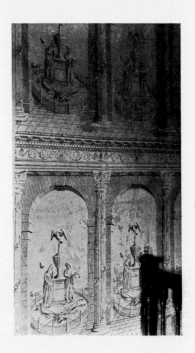

of brightish color in the center, but for the most part the colors were quiet, and the two or three outer rows were dark or black to give strength to the tones.

But the hooked, or the drawn-in rugs, two names for the same thing, are the domestic Wiltons of New England. Many beautiful rugs of this sort are found in Vermont. Made on burlap by the same method as the white counterpanes with candle wicking decorations, they called for every bit of artistic genius the housewife possessed. Some of the handsomer large ones have been disposed of in recent years for fabulous prices.

### COLONIAL JOURNEYS

It was many years after the settlement of these shores before anything fairly resembling a road existed. Finally, the Great and General Court of Massachusetts passed an act to build a road twelve miles west into the wilderness, " That being as far," the act recited, " as anyone could ever wish to go." The first method of travel was, of course, over the Indian trails and by horseback, as soon as the colonies had developed a little. It is a question whether there is any method superior even at the present time, provided one can be sure of pleasant weather. Winding along into the dappling shadows beneath the trees of a primeval forest, coming out now and then into open spaces, was a pleasure shared by all our ancestors into the dim ages of romance. If there was a lady on the pillion she was obliged both for safety and by custom to throw her arms about the cavalier. The superiority of this means of travel becomes apparent over any modern device. A horse requires no wider path than a man, and a journey alone of any great distance begets an intimate acquaintance between the rider and his good beast.

But with the introduction of vehicles by the wealthy the old simple custom passed away, and as time went on the stage-coach came in.

Miss Mary Emmons has supplied me with some suggestions and quotations from which I incorporate some matters in this book.

Sedan chairs in the towns, and chaises in town and country became available. The stage, however, was supposed to be the last word in civilization. The taverns sprang up rapidly on the stage routes. At first they were licensed with strict laws forbidding dancing, singing and the use of tobacco. Later these regulations fell into abeyance or were repealed and the taverns became the centers of hospitality for the traveler and the resident.

The innkeepers were often the most influential men of the town. It is related of the innkeeper at Bennington, Vermont, that he declined to give a dinner to a traveler who came to that town on the day of the Battle of Bennington, because every good man should be in that fight. The traveler rejoined that he had ridden forty miles to reach the battlefield as a delegate from the Continental Congress. The innkeeper was the repository for all the news, both local and general, and when the stage drew up at his door he was a person to whom the hat was doffed with great respect. The stage driver was the proverbial jolly fellow and magnified his office. Many old mile-stones yet mark the way of old post roads which developed from the Indian trails.

The old turnpikes are yet bordered by many a hostelry that once resounded with laughter and teemed with guests. When the route between Providence and Boston was established the Providence *Gazette* had this item: " We were rattled from Providence to Boston in four hours and fifty minutes. If any one wants to go faster he may send to Kentucky and charter a streak of lightning." The fare for this trip was three dollars. Nor was stage-coaching at all in the nature of recreation, except for the hardy.

A person who had made such a journey was like the writer of Holy Writ, " he could tell all his bones." The jolts were a fine treatment for a sluggish liver, and those who lived through the journey arrived well exercised for the bountiful meal that awaited them.

The family trip to market was also a great event and often occupied a considerable period. The teamsters at the foot of a great hill would couple their teams and help one another to the crest. It was on this account

largely that villages grew up on the tops of some of the highest hills in New England. Besides that, in a sparsely settled country the people desired to have wide views. It gave a sense of fellowship if they could see from their homes the spire of a distant village. Thus the marketing trips were great social events especially in the winter when there was more leisure. Many neighbors participated.

The journey was made in pungs, deep laden with produce of the farm. Firkins of butter and lard, kegs of maple syrup, beans, cheese and knitted goods made by the women, and a medley of other products lay in intimate association beneath the fur robes. The housewife added a " mitchen-box " of home-cooked food. The ride became a moving picnic. Rural wit flashed back and forth on the crisp air and many an acquaintance begun under such circumstances became still more intimate by the long evenings at the tavern, where the travelers stopped for the night.

The produce, on arriving at market, was bartered for such articles of luxury as were not produced at home. It was necessary to have a good memory as one could not telephone every five minutes. The technical phrase " a market town " came into use by the location, here and there, of towns scattered at about such distances as would make it possible for travelers in this manner to reach them.

It was owing to this circumstance that such towns were all of about the same size and importance. It was many years before the important city overshadowed its rivals. A single town, perhaps now decadent, sent into the Revolutionary War twice as many men as could be spared today. The dignity and importance of a local center was emphasized and the leaders in such towns developed to such a point of capacity and dignity that they felt themselves the equal of the best in the land.

### A BACKWARD GLANCE

Had we followed the itinerant schoolmaster in his wanderings from week to week or the traveling shoemaker or the parson who looked in for a call and in accordance with the old-time hospitality was urged to stay for a " bite " we should have had an opportunity to see varied arrangements of serving food, fully as interesting as the modern course dinner with its multiplicity of devices. We might have sat at a plain board laid on trestles, a relic of Saxon days, or a " long table " where both sides were occupied and not one, as was the ancient custom, or a " drawing table," which was really an extension table as it truly needed to be in those hospitable days. Had we taken a meal at a " chair table," which could be converted from one article to another, we might have had premonition, not altogether alluring, of some of our present combination furniture so fearfully and wonderfully made. Or we might have been confused by the intricacies of the " hundred leg table " which could be attached to hold the flaps at either end and so accommodate a large number of persons. A portion of one of these tables still in existence is over seven feet wide. They were made, like all sensible things, to fit a need as in the case of one of most curious form, called " three tables forming a horseshoe for the benefit of the fire."

The table covering went through a change in name and form before our present white damask became common. The cover was called board cloth, and was trimmed, when means permitted, with lace, and richly embroidered in colors. The napkins were of the same style and much prized.

The lack of table utensils and the peculiarity of those in use would have embarrassed us, like an invitation to eat with chop sticks. Like Penelope, suffering the agonies of breaking an egg at an English breakfast table, we should scarcely have known the knack of the proprieties, and we certainly could not have eaten with our forks.

The table ware of the Pilgrim Fathers was meager. Governor Winthrop had sent to him in 1633 the first fork used in America and the note accompanying it was, " A fork for the useful applycation of which I leave to your discretion." We are not told what purpose the fork was made to serve.

" The standing salt " was often the most important piece of plate and, as in England, the social standing of guests was determined by the posi-

tion of the seat above or below the salt. Is this why the spilling of salt between two people assumed such a significance?

The table furnishings of the New England planters were chiefly trenchers, square blocks of wood whittled out by hand. Often only one graced the board of an entire family. Woe be to the modern theory of germs and the intricate methods of housekeeping! These wooden dishes gave way to pewter ware, and this, in its turn, about the time of the Revolutionary War, to porcelain.

### INDEPENDENCE

The joy of achievement! Who has not felt it in a greater or less measure? Who, indeed, but the fawning dependent creature who is fond of quoting " The Lord will provide "? as He does indeed by the painstaking, unselfish labor of some one who is ready to carry the burden. In the days of our forefathers there was not so much temptation to *lean,* for the very nature of the work necessary to sustain life prompted independence. Was it not in a way a struggle for " the survival of the fittest "? It was taken for granted, not argued or timidly requested by faltering parents, that children should assume their rightful share of the day's duties. Much of the boys' spare time was given to chopping wood, carrying water and feeding the horses, while the girls no less employed the time to their own and others' advantage by spinning, sewing, weaving, wiping dishes or sweeping. These habits bore fruit by producing sturdy, independent, thrifty men and women. The sternness and simplicity of their struggle for existence rooted in them the principles that made them men, not weaklings. Was not a young man in those days spared to a certain extent the often harrowing stage when he must decide whether he would be " doctor, lawyer, merchant, thief "? when every man must be his own provider and it was clear that he must do the " next thing."

If one now is so fortunate as to possess the " wherewithal," the necessity for independence has relaxed, and a weak character results. Machinery has superseded handwork and we know that to some extent this is disadvantageous.   Yet the traits of our forefathers can be traced in many directions.   The same self-respect, courage, determination and ability are apparent in the magnificent achievements of today — the tunnels, the vast irrigation works in the West reclaiming the waste lands, the canal with its great locks and dams, the construction of which seems almost superhuman — these and many other things show that our ancestors did not struggle in vain.

### A RAISING

When iron was rare and valuable, it was usual to frame the house without it.   Mortice and tenon were used to make all connections and these were pinned with wood.   The frame of the entire side would fasten together lying on the ground.   When all was ready, invitations were sent far and wide and it was regarded as the duty, as well as the pleasure, of every one summoned to lend his presence.   The entire side of heavy timbers was lifted at once and held in place while another was raised to match it.   Then the young and agile men received the roof pieces and at length with appropriate ceremonies one of the more daring sat upon the ridge pole and led the cheers.   Thus the work of many months hastened to immediate completion.

Merry girls flitted about and distributed the refreshments provided by the host — cider, doughnuts, cheese, and sometimes a formal " raising " supper was served.

### THE TIME OF DAY

We, with our watches and numerous clocks, are hardly able to imagine ourselves without any adequate method of keeping time.

Our fathers welcomed the tall clocks and counted them as objects worthy of rich ornament and scrupulous care.   Before clocks could be afforded men became quite adept at estimating the time of day merely by looking at the sun.

The almanac derived its great importance from the lack of time-keepers.  Twice on every fair day, at sunrise and sunset, an isolated family could

check the time roughly by the almanac. I remember that my grandfather could tell the noon hour within ten minutes by a glance at the sun. Persons of a very regular habit also have a time-keeper in their stomachs.

Then, also, some had sun-dials, but as there were only two days in the year when the dial was accurate, a more or less involved problem was necessary to ascertain the precise time. It is, perhaps, owing to their habit of following the sun that our fathers rose so early in the summer. We joke about the early hours of retiring in the country. It is probable, however, that city dwellers sleep longer than their country cousins. If the settler went to bed with the chickens, he also arose with them and his hours of activity of mind and body were greater than our own.

In winter it was, of course, necessary to take breakfast and supper by candle light or by the " hearth-fire's ruddy glow." The winter, however, was not the season when important labors pressed upon the settler. Aside from the care of his beasts, the ploughing out of the roads after the snows and the getting up of the annual store of wood, his out-door duties were intermitted.

Many of his winter days were given to making plain and simple articles of furniture, for which we are now ready to pay nearly their weight in silver.

Another means of time reckoning was by the hour glass, but this required some one to watch it and turn it over the moment the sand had run through. Hour glasses were therefore especially appropriate for desks where people worked regularly, as the parson or the professional writer.

The term " sparking " to designate that ancient Saturday night custom of calling on a sweetheart, was probably derived from the sparking lamp. An open but deep vessel of glass had poured into it such a quantity of oil by the watchful mother as she considered proper to burn during the young man's call. On the oil was placed a floating wick which gave a dim light, it is true, but probably enough to suit the persons concerned. The mother therefore had in the sparking lamp a means of showing her opinion of the suitor. If he were a young man likely to do well in the world and of good character she allowed her hand to let the oil flow more generously than otherwise.

It was not considered proper for a caller to remain after the oil was exhausted. It formed a variable time-keeper. We may picture the anxious look of the swain at the condition of the lamp when it was brought into the best room.

## XLIII. THE FUTURE OF VERMONT

WHILE people cannot move mountains they can do almost anything else to make or mar a state. The people of Vermont control the future of Vermont in a physical as well as in a social sense.

The population of Vermont was not many years since of one class and one race. The state was a fine example of that unity of people which used to be counted an important social advantage. It was thought that here in the north was one region at least where early American traditions could be carried out by a people descended from British ancestry. Nowhere except in the mountain states of the south was the population so largely native.

It is a darling dream, — that of a country of one race, one religion, one condition of comfort without wealth. But it is a dream from which Vermont has awakened with something of surprise and perhaps of sorrow. It is true, and easily seen to be true, looking backward, that not all the people were worthy and wise. There were here and there marks of neglect as one journeyed through the state. Antiquated methods of farming were common.

But that spirit of independence and self-sufficiency which had become a second nature of her people, derived from her revolutionary experience, had been depended upon to work out a social condition of the most attractive rural type. What might have eventuated it is perhaps useless to speculate here. For the mark of every sane mind is to take account of conditions,

not of theories. Vermont is in a state of rapid flux when viewed by the long vision of history. To a considerable extent it is becoming a new French Canadian province. How far the influx of the prolific French families is to modify old Vermont one would be a daring prophet to declare. It is impossible to forecast with any degree of probability the extent to which the French immigration will continue; it is not possible to know whether the present numerical superiority of a French over a Yankee family will be maintained; it is not possible to say just what the social reaction of the mixture of races will be.

If we glance at the history of French Canada we observe first of all that its people are conservative to an extreme degree. That conservatism marks the French character in the old world as well. Outside of Paris the French are an exceedingly stiff and unvarying people, in their work and their ideals. There is no valid reason for supposing that the French nature will change in any important degree. True, the impulse of change which has brought about this French immigration may be thought to indicate that the immigrant is more receptive of new ideas than his congener who remained behind on the Canadian home acres. But the hope of bettering one's self financially may not mark any awakening to new aspects of life in general.

The conservatism of the French Canadian may prove a valuable asset on the American side of the line, where society seems at times in danger of being shifted too fast and in a wrong direction. At the basis of any great and durable state lies that love of the land, and that continuance on it which has marked the Kelt in all generations. A stable farm life is the necessary condition for the progress of any nation. As soon as the farming population become restive, and on slight excuse, or no excuse at all, leave behind their ancient occupation and seek a new one, so soon is a state completely upset and in extreme peril. It was this change that overthrew Italy in the classic period. It appears to all careful students that a people who will stick to the land, through good season and bad season, who will carry on farm work whether it offers the highest rewards or not are the greatest asset of any state and the necessary foundation of any state.

The author once tried to purchase from a Kelt a farm. It was not ancestral in the Kelt's family. The offer gradually rose to nearly three times the intrinsic value, as the farm was desired by the prospective purchaser for ulterior reasons. But no amount of persuasion would avail, and we are sure that the offer if doubled again would still have been declined. The owner was not a good farmer, nor a very diligent man. But he simply clung to his land. The love of the Irish for a piece of land is proverbial. We are bound to say that the trait is profoundly beneficial to society at large. It will be a sad day when men cease to joy in the ownership of land and acquire the tenant habit. If the French people who are buying Vermont farms remain unchanged in their habit of clinging to their lands these immigrants aside from any other merits or demerits that may mark them, will prove ultimately good citizens. The stabilizing effect of acre ownership is superior to any other known force in society. It is not likely that what has ever been true in this regard will change.

How far the similar persistence in the French immigrants in maintaining their own language will go is somewhat uncertain. But the tendency is to the adoption of English in a far greater degree than in Canada, for the reason that whereas in Canada the French populations are solid bodies, generally, they are in Vermont naturally scattered here and there among English people. We may well believe also that the predominant English race will force, through schools and courts and trade relations the final and general adoption of English speech. Otherwise Vermont would become a state with communities growing up here and there cut off by alien speech from the body of the nation's people — always a danger, often a catastrophe. We saw in Canada during the great war the remarkable phenomenon of a French people going grudgingly to the aid of their motherland France. The cause of this unwillingness for war is doubtless assignable in part to other reasons than the almost hermitlike life of segregation marking rural French Canada, but that parochial self-sufficiency, fostered by their speech, is yet a partial reason for the general unwillingness to enter on the rescue of France.

We are perhaps safe in believing that the present vigorous movement of Americanization will not be turned aside successfully by the French immigrant.

Turning to another community to reinforce our main thought, we see in parts of old fashioned rural Pennsylvania a persistence of habit that has been a vast source of strength to the state and the nation. The descendants of German and Dutch settlers, especially the former, have by their steady continuance in devoting themselves to the soil established a rural community unrivalled in many of its merits by any in this country. For we must never forget that not genius, nor even learning, is the mainstay of the state, but the continual efforts of the average man, age after age, to subdue the earth and rule over it.

Going back now to Vermont, we find it a state dependent more than most upon the undiscouraged efforts of the farmer who tills his own farm of moderate size, keeps wild game from swarming down from the hills, keeps the roads and the schools open, and goes on steadily holding society together, consciously or unconsciously waiting for a better day. So long as every boy looks upon himself as a possible future President of the United States America will be secure. It is the taming of the world in waiting hope that makes the future secure.

If some deplore the taking over of Vermont acres by the French people we can only reply to them that if Americans abandon their birthright it is far better that other peoples should take the land than that it relapse into a wilderness. For the truth must be faced; there are not enough farmer's boys left in Vermont who are willing to work the ancestral acres. The future of the state must therefore be worked out by the old inhabitants, together with the immigrants, to save the fair hills to use and beauty. There are happily a remnant of the old stock who love their old homes and their occupation. They have produced the Morgan horse; they have demonstrated the possible profitableness of hill farms; they have shown the feasibility of combining hand work with head work so as to produce a generation as far removed as possible from the peasant condition. Of course it is conceivable that Vermont may become predominantly foreign. But even that condition is not as sad to contemplate as the giving up of a good acre to grow wild again — a sight more pregnant of disaster than any other. The reaction of American ideals is very potent. We are hopeful concerning the future of Vermont. We believe that as soon as the unrest left by the great war has been calmed, the return to the land on the part of a select class of old Americans may be hoped for.

Meanwhile there is work for all in developing the state of Vermont. Idle hands are so only from preference. What we hope is the only fine stimulus for what we do. The hopes of nations and of communities may rise and fall, but in the main there is advance in the conditions of country life. We see also in the diversity of Vermont's physical resources a reason for hope. A prairie state is naturally given over largely to one sort of occupation and one main crop.

The very diversity of Vermont's surface tends to that greatest advantage of the agriculturist — mixed farming. When to this varied sort of farming we add the manufacturing which the lumber, granite and marble of Vermont stimulates, we obtain a healthful society, mutually reacting, each part to the advantage of the other.

In the midst of this necessary attention to labor, if the Vermonter does not forget the winning quality of his state upon the tourist he will do well. What attracts a tourist is not so much an occasional center of thrift, as a general appearance of well-being over the entire countryside. Of course we all enthusiastically admit that a fertile, well cared for, well-watered, well-wooded countryside, with grazing herds, neat farm buildings and fair roads, is the most delightful vision that bursts on a weary mankind. It calls us back to paradise, or what is better, to making a paradise of our own. The original paradise was merely a sample. Men were driven out of it in order that after repeated and age-long experiment they might erect a newer paradise, of which they would become careful, since they themselves erected it, and knew its worth.

Vermont for its future will need, at least it will be greatly helped by,

the admiration and enthusiasm of the outsider. The people from far cities who travel in Vermont will at last enthuse the last Vermonter over his own state. There is need of this inspirational work though perhaps the Vermonter may repudiate the idea. He has only to be asked to make up a tally of the Vermonters who have departed from the state of their birth. The country swarms with them. They love their state, but they love it from afar; they sing its praises but they no longer see its beauties except at rare intervals. Therefore there are many Vermonters who need to be kept in Vermont, men who do not know that they already possess whatever of paradise is still left for men. The winters of Vermont seem to some of its people a grim answer to such an assertion. But woe to the race that comes to regard cold weather as the enemy of man, or a ban on his development or enjoyment. Various hotels are already teaching Vermonters that their winters are one of the State's great attractions. It is said by hotel men south of Vermont that they cannot depend upon steady cold weather for winter sports, and that it is in Vermont that they find most accessibly a steady cold in a region of natural beauty. It may be that the winter climate of Vermont, which has been thought by many shrinking emigrants a handicap, will in time come to be regarded as her best feature, for health, rest, beauty and finally for fertility. For on the last depends largely the quickly springing grass, always greenest under a snowdrift. At this very point it is important to meet squarely the popular and erroneous notion that cold weather counts against a climate. To begin with, it is true that in no part of our country do people suffer so much from the cold as in the South. The writer never came so near perishing from cold as in Florida in December, because he was not prepared to resist cold. The people of the South not requiring good houses seldom build them. Not finding the necessity of thrift they are less formed in habits of sound economy. South of Mason and Dixon's line commercial credits average much longer than north of that line.

That is only another way of illustrating the effect of climate on character. It has always required cold weather to tone men up. Cold weather is a wonderful stimulus to architecture, to invention, to manufactures, to community of effort and interest.

Let the inert, the anemic, the drones seek the life of the South if they will. A little visit to a warmer district in winter may prove a reasonable and pleasing relaxation for a Vermonter. But any one who investigates will learn that the work which sets the world forward is done at home, by the Vermonter, who cannot relax and labor at the same time.

The influence of climate on ideas is a subject that will bear more study than it has ever received. But let the Vermonter ask himself this one question: What will the future of my children be in the South, as compared with their future in the state of their birth? There is but one answer. Independence and activity will be nurtured best at home.

But the encouragement which the Vermonter needs, in many instances, to stay at home, rather than emigrate, is still further given by pointing out to him attractions of his state which he has failed to recognize. This statement seems extremely conceited. But judged by figures it does not prove so. The Vermonter continues to leave home and does not come back. Hence the advantage of an occasional poet-capitalist who settles in the state and combs out the beauty of a countryside. Travel, if the traveler is awake, certainly tends to disseminate good ideas, and the Vermonter who travels forth and returns again has learned by comparison the advantages of his home state. It would be too tedious to mention the many persons who like the Evarts family of Windsor have held and developed their home acres, although the keenness of their minds has called them forth to fight successfully in the nation's more populous centers. There are those who believe William M. Evarts was the best intellect of his day. He was molded by the first Vermont influences and he never forgot his debt to his native state.

No doubt in the process of time other men will arise to render their nation illustrious, and to give dignity to its native manhood. Meantime let us rejoice in the opportunity Vermont has to produce such men. Most of all let us indulge the hope that the conditions that rendered an Evarts possible will continue, guarded jealously by the loyal Vermonter. That loyal

Vermonter will know that the only state worth saving is a state capable of yielding both beauty and strength.

The future of Vermont is therefore, even on the physical side, dependent on the sort of men who are to form her inhabitants.

The conservation of her forests to prevent floods, the steady and harmonious development of all her resources so that no one development kills another, these must come about through a wise citizenship who intend to live all their lives with Vermont as their front yard.

### THE VERMONTER OUTSIDE VERMONT

There have sprung up, in various parts of our country, Vermont societies, devoted to retelling old tales of the state their members love, to renewing boyhood associations, to binding all concerns of life to sentiment, and to concerting measures for the good of Vermont. We must look largely to such societies to do necessary things for the state, which will perhaps otherwise remain undone.

Living out of Vermont members of these societies are able to gain a truer perspective, perhaps, of the State and its needs, than are the people within its own borders.

These societies, when once they have seriously studied the matter, will know what must attract the general public to Vermont, and the scattering of facts about the state will prove of great advantage. For Vermont only needs the truth told about her in order to be loved. Without meaning to be invidious we are obliged to admit that certain western states have spread abroad golden propaganda which those induced by this means to settle in those states have not always found borne out by the facts.

There is enough natural beauty in Vermont to induce admiration, and it is in part the self appointed but humble though joyful mission of this book to point out a few of those beauties. There is enough natural wealth, good climate, and enough of all that renders human life worth while, within the limits of Vermont, to afford abundant material to all who wish to set the facts forth. The serious and unhappy fact is that we in America have often held cheap things in esteem, and ignored what was of most worth. A fair and fruitful state, within three or four hours of salt water, within two hours of great cities, set among hills, dotted with lakes, green with the wealth of forest and field, rich in corn and flocks, romantic in its traditions, proud of its history and altogether attractive economically and aesthetically, such a state cannot much longer fail to be appreciated at its true and great worth. We bespeak success to all Vermont Societies and wisdom to all their efforts in behalf of the most homelike of all states.

Indeed this book will appeal more to the Vermonter who lives far from his native state than to him who remains in the old home. The non-resident needs most some reminder of the old home. A dealer in pictures, in the city of Denver, once said: " What I want is pictures in my window such that people will stop before them and *weep*." He wanted a call in the picture, to the eye, that would bring back, in a rush of sentiment, all the memories of childhood. The brow of the hill around which the road curved, and where the maples waved in the wind, the cottage under the elm; the brook by the foot of the hill; the bars let down as the cows came home; the home turn into the dear old front yard, and all the thousand nameless charms that overflow the heart and make life something better than a tread-mill. And is that not what we all crave? We recognize, though we may be too proud or cynical to admit it, the value of sentiment. We love the calls that are most human, and we look with longing even at scenes that recall hardship.

When the last account is cast up and we forget all about the price of hay and corn we shall still hold in dearest memory the picture of the boy perched high on the load of hay, and the tugging horses as they rush across the barn bridge through the great doors to escape the shower. We shall remember the husking, the many lanterns, the great mows of hay as the background, the vast piles of yellow corn, the eagerness of the young faces in the flickering light!

It is better than pelf, better than glory, more lasting than any dazzling success. For it is life in its universal aspect, its hearty honest hopeful struggle, its helpful kindness, its halo of neighborly trust and good will over all.

In simplicity, in homely comfort, in true warm friendship, in helping one's neighbor, in the hope of sowing, in the joy of harvest, in the glow of morning and the quiet of twilight glow over the Western hills we leave our dear state — till another occasion.

## XLIV.  RED LETTER DAYS IN VERMONT

ABOUT the time the century came in we lived a summer in St. Johnsbury.  The horse we hired was Old Harry, the " old " being an adjective of endearment, not of moral opprobrium.  Old Harry was a Morgan — the horse whose Arab strain, developed for lightness, quickness, and bottom, has given us the finest equine known for hilly regions.

At first the steep hills were frightful, especially their descent.  But after a few experiences, we found that Old Harry, when given his head, for he was never checked, would scramble up and scamper down the boldest slopes safely and expeditiously.  He was old, yet he went farther in a day than the standards set for a city horse.  Old Harry never seemed to feel a weakness.  He showed us the beauties of a large part of Vermont.  By-roads were his joy.  His careful attention to business, his good temper and good heart, have left an ineffaceable impression, which is blended in memory with the beautiful experiences of the summer.

Under a birch grove we gave Old Harry his oats at noon, and ate with gusto what our dear landlady had prepared for us.  Over in the highlands of Concord we came upon wonderful clumps of beeches, birches, and maples.  Along the shores of the Connecticut we passed a farm with three thousand maples in its sugar orchard!  In the higher valleys were many little farms, each with its little wedge-shaped corn house, its shop, its sugar house, and its barn.  We found the air always cool in the morning and the evening; almost always by six o'clock one needed an overcoat when driving.  Only from ten to four the power of the sun made us linger in the shady ways to revel in the flickering lights, and to watch the little wild life flitting or scampering around us.  Danvilleward and beyond are many high but fair round hills, as smoothly covered with grass or corn as any meadow. Rank on rank of hills rise to the eye.    First come the green, then blue, then purple, and what is beyond is only a dreamy mist that might veil some greater beauty.

In the region about Vergennes, during another summer, we used to cross the broad plains which stretch for miles, their roads as straight as if across a prairie.    The fences which bordered those roads were the picturesque Virginia rail fence, angular, zigzag, with woodbine, ivy, or wild rose rising above the rails at the angles.    There was no lack of symmetrical elms, of stately old brick houses, of meandering streams, while always to the east the wall of mountains rose, challenging rather than forbidding.

Or on another day, instead of keeping to the plains, we pulled ourselves carefully up the great rock headlands of Champlain, north of Burlington. In the morning light, in quiet hours, the Adirondacks stand out boldly, bounding the western shore.    They reminded us of the starker crags that bound the Salton Sea in California.    There is not elsewhere in the East any such extent of beauty, in broad effects combining water and mountain, as we see when looking across Lake Champlain.

Not all of our days were spent in far journeys, however.    Some were pleasantly passed in excursions for berries and in the simple act of picking them.

At the edge of the " cut-down " the wild strawberries were very sweet — the conical, deep red berry with seeds lying outside.    We gathered not only enough for shortcake, but a surplus to preserve.    It was the hottest sort of pleasure, for we had to pick when the grass was dry and the June sun baking hot.    Picking raspberries was more comfortable, for we gathered them by the roadside on overcast days.    But blackberrying was an unmixed delight.    With two large pails and small picking dishes and our luncheon, we started up the mountainside in the August morning and never returned until the gloaming.    It was part of the ritual not only to heap the pails but to fill the picking dishes besides.    In the high pastures, under the fleeting clouds, we looked out on the valley, our little world, spread below.    The days were never too long.

Sometimes a party of some size was made up, and as the picking proceeded the conversation did not lag, though we learned that the still pickers carried home the heaviest pails. Berry picking allows of almost any topic of conversation. The theme of the future career of boy and girl was common. With the somewhat sardonic humor of one farmer, who opined that Fred, a somewhat erratic boy, " would do well if he kept out of jail," there was mingled the pride and hope of some farmer's wife that Charles would grow to be a college professor. Sometimes the picker's luck reminded one of the wider channels of life. A clump of bushes which no one else had found was laden with big luscious fruit, and there the pails filled rapidly. Then one might wander far with only an occasional berry for reward.

In the days after the haying, the youths and elders occasionally made a general picnic with the children and went a-berrying too. It is said that when the hands of youth and maiden touched, as each, by chance, of course, worked on the same bush, life partnerships were made. On these picnics old married folks renewed their youth and their wooing, too. Among the pleasantest days of our lives were those vacations from the strenuous toil of town in the mountain pastures. It was " seeing Vermont " under the most delightful auspices.

Occasionally we made up a party to ascend the higher shoulders of the mountains. There we camped before a roaring fire, our feet toward it, in a lean-to of saplings and evergreen boughs. When we slept we thrust our legs into bags to keep warm. Our fast was broken with the food we had taken with us, together with highbush cranberries which grow far up on the mountain side. We sweetened them with maple sugar which we had brought along. With an appetite sharpened by hunger after our sharp climb, we had a dinner such as no fashionable café can furnish. So long as we retain this youthful zest,

> " What have years to bring,
> But larger floods of love and lights,
> And sweeter songs to sing? "

One picnic day was passed quite differently. In North Danville stood an ancient cottage, shown opposite. Here with a coterie of friends we roamed about, admiring the quaintness of the house. The tame calves came to be fondled and fed. Dreamy air surrounded us. Rest seemed the normal occupation of man. The cottage was Vermont personified. It was simple, honest, kindly, cozy, and independent. As the past flowed into the present, sentiment claimed us, and this little poem grew:

> *Cottage and elm began their day together;*
> *The one is breaking in the century's blast;*
> *Looming triumphant over wind and weather,*
> *The other shields its comrade to the last.*
>
> *Five generations in their home-nest here,*
> *Beneath the tree, have waxed to manhood's might;*
> *Where still the boughs caress the ruin sere,*
> *The sun with lingering kiss still bids good-night.*
>
> *Grant us the gift of lengthening days,*
> *More winning and more mellow year by year;*
> *Give us the home-hearth with its cheering blaze,*
> *And crown us with such comradeship as here!*

Seven years after that delightful day the old house had burned and the great elm had fallen in a storm. Musing on the twin disasters, we added these lines as a sequel:

> *The flame has claimed the relics of my rhyme;*
> *The earth has called the elm back to her breast;*
> *I ponder in the ruins, past my prime,*
> *Upon the mysteries of change and rest.*
>
> *But other suns will raise up elms more fair,*
> *Beneath which better homes will rise;*
> *And stronger hearts will weave the life-thread there,*
> *And better minds will worthier rhymes devise.*

Indeed, humanity seems to divide into those who mourn the past and those who shape the future — a worthier and a more healthful task.

# INDEX

# INDEX OF PICTURES

# INDEX OF PICTURES